EXPLORING THE LAND

BY SHANE BENNETT & KIM FELDER WITH STEVE HAWTHORNE

DISCOVERING WAYS FOR
UNREACHED PEOPLE
TO FOLLOW CHRIST

Caleb
PROJECT

ISBN: 1-932329-05-6

Copyright © 2003, 1995 by Caleb Project

Published by Caleb Project
10 West Dry Creek Circle
Littleton, CO 80120-4413

Printed in the United States of America

Cover photography by Michael Staub and Patty Fraats. Special thanks to Pioneers for the use of their photographs on pages 9, 12, 21, 27, 96, 115, 117, 120, and 123.

Contents

Foreword

Living in this century is like being glued to a breathtaking, suspense-filled story. The Evil One looks tougher than the Triumphant One, but we have all read the end of the story. We know that tens of thousands among all nations are indeed going to bow to Christ and become adopted, worshiping members of his family!

God is going to use someone. Who? Obviously, those who are available. But availability isn't enough. Far too many people – having moved to a city where the inhabitants have no idea that God has visited the earth – make little happen that counts for eternity. Why?

Over the last twenty years we have seen, in answer to prayer, a great number of world Christians take up residence among Muslims, Hindus, Buddhists, and other pagans of secular cities. Countries are no longer "closed" because we no longer depend on a missionary visa. From Morocco to Brunei, "tentmakers" have infiltrated for Christ.

But in many cases, the devil is laughing. In our enthusiasm to go where Christ is not named, most ambassadors for Christ have focused so much on their entry strategy that after settling in, they find that they don't know how to make disciples. Many are not learning the languages of their adopted people well enough to read the newspaper or teach the Bible.

That is why *Exploring the Land* has been compiled. Caleb Project is committed to helping us keep the Great Commandment by not only loving God with our hearts, but also with our minds. They realize that we are not called to soothe the evangelical conscience by doing outreach, but to actually reach people by making disciples. *Exploring the Land* is about bearing God's kind of fruit – fruit that will last. It is about seeing people who are totally out of touch with God's Church become an integral part of it – worshipers who worship in spirit and truth (see John 4:23-24). And it is about glorifying God by building communities of believers who love God and each other, and who reproduce the church in their culture.

Oh, how I wish I and my co-workers would have had such a guide book earlier in our careers. What a difference it might have made. Read it over and over. Review it with your co-workers. Get points clarified until it is user friendly. Caleb Project staff can be called upon for help. Turn *Exploring the Land* into a personal manual as you write notes in it and eventually produce a version for your own situation.

Remember, *Exploring the Land* is a primer. It is an introduction into a new world of *savoir-faire*. Take these ideas and methods seriously and you will be well on your way to knowing what you're doing and why. Welcome to the deeply satisfying adventure of becoming an insider.

Dr. Greg Livingstone, Frontiers

Preface

God is accelerating the advance of his kingdom with unprecedented speed. Godless ideologies are crumbling. Churches are growing and multiplying, many in unexpected locations. And believers worldwide are rallying to God's banner, proclaiming the gospel to the ends of the earth in ever increasing numbers.

While the message goes forth with greater volume to more and more people, we still find whole peoples among whom the Church has yet to take hold. What is needed? More missionaries? Yes. Better contextualization of the message? Probably. More prayer? Definitely. All of these are appropriate responses in these days. But something else is often overlooked.

As we step out to follow Jesus, taking the gospel to all people, the questions that quickly rise to the top of our lists almost exclusively have to do with ourselves. Once we have chosen a people to minister to, we begin to ask "How shall I maintain a viable presence in a foreign country?" "How will I fund this work?" "What language shall I learn?" These are all valid questions requiring honest answers. Unfortunately, we often limit our investigations to such questions that fall under the cover question, "How will I proclaim the message to these people?"

We need to lift our eyes beyond ourselves to ask, "How will these people follow Christ?" That, after all, remains our eternal, compelling goal. Effective

How will these unreached peoples follow Christ?

communication is a means. Accurate translation of the Bible is another means. Even conversion is a means to the end that a person, and a remnant of every people, becomes a follower of Christ. We must ask questions that will unveil this wonderful mystery. "How will a new believer in this people group worship?" "What will an inviting, relevant church look like for them?" Essentially, "How will this unreached people find God's way to follow Christ?"

Since 1988, Caleb Project has been training and sending short-term research teams to ask these questions. More than 200 people have served on nearly forty teams ranging from the Middle East to South East Asia. Yet the need for research of this type far outpaces the number of teams being sent. This need, along with repeated requests for materials that will equip others to conduct such research, has led to the production of this manual.

Who should read *Exploring the Land?*

Mission Agency Personnel

> *We here in Youth With A Mission, India have greatly benefited from the research and strategic input published by Caleb Project. Two of our teams have extensively used their reports. We have found that hundreds of hours of research (necessary to begin work among newly targeted groups) was done for us, saving months of pre-ministry work. We commend the hard work of Caleb Project staff and volunteers, and appreciate their partnership with us in the extension of God's kingdom among the unreached peoples of the world.*

> – Assistant Director, YWAM Frontier Missions Center, Pune, India

Mission agency personnel should read this manual as they seek God for fresh organizational direction. *Exploring the Land* will help you practically approach the opening of new fields and the deployment of new missionaries. Unreached people are all the rage, but how do you know where to begin? Recruiting and sending a research team will help you set a specific course of action as you begin work among unreached peoples. Participation on a short-term research team can be used to initiate or aid in the recruitment of new workers. Their experience can provide potential recruits with an insightful introduction to your agency. Research teams are also great tools to mobilize constituent churches. As churches provide and care for team members, they receive vision, ownership, and insight for prayer. Finally, this manual is an invaluable tool to put in the hands of your veteran workers, showing them ways to unravel particularly unknowable aspects of their target culture.

Missions Pastors

I believe Caleb Project is on the cutting edge of God's global mission strategy for our generation. The research among hidden people groups and subsequent networking of information is a tremendous help to the work of global missions. Also, the efforts of mobilizing local churches to become more intentional and focused in their particular mission strategy may prove to be the emphasis that "tips the scales" in favor of completing the task of world evangelization .... My exposure to the needs of people in southeast Asia has significantly impacted my vision for world evangelization, and subsequently the mission thrust of our local church.

– Pastor Gregg Parris, Union Chapel Ministries

Missions pastors should use this manual to give renewed life and effectiveness to their church's short- and long-term mission efforts. Short-term research teams can be integrated into your current missions focus. They will make a lasting difference for you and your local church. Short-term missionaries will have an experience that counts, both for them and for the people they work among. Too often, short-term missionaries feel that they have simply spent a summer somewhere, rather than having invested it. They also feel disconnected from their local church. Sending a short-term team from a local fellowship, while challenging, reconnects missions and the church. Whether the team joins your missionaries on the field or investigates a newly adopted unreached people, we have found that integrated efforts build stronger interest and involvement for the entire church.

Novice and Seasoned Missionaries

On behalf of our church planting team, I am writing to express my deep appreciation for the research you have done. We on the scene are often so involved in the details of church planting, that we sometimes overlook the big picture. What you have done has really helped us to regain our perspective. Our team is in the process of studying your finished document and wrestling with its implications for our church planting efforts.

– Long-term church planter, Bangkok, Thailand

Exploring the Land is a helpful tool for both novice and seasoned missionaries. New recruits can use the methods described here to focus their efforts on a specific people and to envision the church they hope to plant. New missionaries may wish to spend their first year exploring the questions this manual presents. Perhaps a team specifically recruited to research your target area would be appropriate. If you have served for years on the mission field, the information

Exploring the Land is a helpful tool for both novice and seasoned missionaries.

discussed here may help you gain insight leading to expanded effectiveness. It may lift your eyes to imagine God doing a work beyond what you have previously dreamed. If this manual blesses you or helps you in any way, it will have been successful. Long-term missionaries are regarded as heroes at Caleb Project.

Auxiliary Materials

Other excellent resources on missiology and ethnography are available to aid you in research and church planting. We recommend the mission study course called *Perspectives On the World Christian Movement*. This course is a prerequisite for all who participate in Caleb Project Research Expeditions. To find out more about *Perspectives,* see the note included in the References.

You may also wish to consider partnering with Caleb Project to address your research needs. Our mandate is to serve the Church for the completion of the Great Commission. We are willing to help with as little as a simple word of advice to as much as multi-team, multi-year partnerships. Contact Caleb Project for further information.

Security Concerns

This manual has been written with the assumption that its readership may include people opposed to the work of God. Therefore, names of certain people and places have been changed to protect individuals and the work in which they are involved. Other security measures have been taken to protect future Caleb Project Research Expeditions.

Acknowledgments

The authors wish to thank a number of individuals whose lives God has used to bring about this manual.

Deb Sanders: Midwife to this manual. Deb helped us say what we wanted to say when we didn't know how and when we had tried and unknowingly failed. Throughout this project Deb has deftly balanced the often contradictory roles of editor and friend. She has stood with us, reminding us to focus, telling us when to breathe and when to push. *Exploring the Land* could not have been delivered by any more sure and caring hands.

Jeleta Eckheart: Charter member of the Caleb Project Research Hall of Fame. Jeleta excelled on the first-ever research team. More recently, she reviewed an early draft of this manual and provided insights which significantly shaped the final product.

Thanks to the professors and missionaries who have been willing to come alongside the efforts of a ragtag band of inexperienced researchers. You have been gracious when we have been proud; you have spoken wisely when we have been humble and attentive.

Thanks to our families and co-workers at Caleb Project whose forbearance and winsome grace have given us the needed encouragement and latitude to finish this project.

Finally, thanks to approximately 150 researchers who have implemented and thereby shaped our research philosophy and method. And thanks to the countless scores of people, from many religions and in many nations, who have befriended our researchers. Though you will likely never read this manual, God knows you and has marked your kindness to strangers in your lands. May he quickly enfold you and your families into his kingdom.

Introduction:
Setting the Scene

History

Caleb Project Research began as an idea in the fertile mind of Steve Hawthorne. In 1981 Steve helped to launch a people group "search" team. This team set off for Taipei, Taiwan to investigate the Chinese working class. Soon afterward, Steve joined the staff of World Christian magazine. There, he proposed that World Christian magazine recruit and send short-term mission teams to gather fresh pictures and stories from unreached areas of the world. While serving the needs of the magazine, young missionary zealots would have an opportunity to build relationships with people beyond the current reach of the gospel. Over the course of three years, four such teams ventured to the Middle East and South Asia, returning with in-depth strategy reports and fodder for several articles in the magazine. In early 1987, the concept moved to Caleb Project. Almost forty teams have been sent out since then. Without a magazine to supply with material, Caleb Project focused on refining the research model that Steve Hawthorne first set forth. A short-term experience was created with lifelong results both for team members and for the people they researched.

The Lineage of Joshua and Caleb

Biblically, we trace our lineage to Joshua and Caleb and their expedition recorded in Numbers 13 and 14. Moses, acting on instructions from God, chose twelve leaders from the nation of Israel to scout out the land God was going to give them. They explored the land, found out what the people and cities were like, then reported back to Moses. We see similarities between this ancient reconnaissance effort and Caleb Project Research Expeditions in four areas.

Similar Assignments

Moses told the scouts to explore the land, not to start conquering it. Likewise, we go to unreached cities to learn about the peoples, not to directly evangelize them.

Similar Reports

We bring back reports similar to Joshua and Caleb's report. While the other ten scouts saw great challenges and wavered, Joshua and Caleb reported honestly on the obstacles and reminded the Israelites of God's promises. We want the reports that we bring back to be unflinchingly honest; we will never gloss over the difficulties missionaries will face in an unreached city. At the same time, our reports are filled with hope that God has wonderful things in store for the peoples of the cities we research.

Similar Audiences

Moses's scouts brought their report back to him and to the assembled nation of Israel. Likewise, Caleb Project researchers bring back an in-depth report tailored for church leaders and others with a long-term commitment to the peoples researched. They also prepare mobilization tools, or "mini-reports" for the church at large which encourage its involvement and facilitate informed prayer (see Appendix II: Caleb Project Resources on page 167).

Similar Vision

Finally, we endeavor to see the world with the vision Joshua and Caleb had. We long to understand and have such an awareness of God's word and his purposes that we see him conquering the giants in the promised land. We want to stand before the Church with faith and join Caleb in proclaiming, "We should by all means go up and take possession of the land, for we can certainly do it" (see Numbers 13:30).

Modern Predecessors

We owe a great deal to the ground-breaking thought of Dr. Donald MacGavran. Dr. MacGavran was among the first to speculate that God may wish to work in line with the unique cultures he had designed. Written off by many, Dr. MacGavran persevered, ultimately reshaping the way missiologists look at the unsaved world. We like to think of our research as "applied MacGavranism," using his thought to develop practical strategies to reach all nations.

We are further indebted to James P. Spradley, whose book *The Ethnographic Interview* has served for nearly twenty years as our guide to the joys and woes of ethnography.

Caleb Project Research results from a knitting together of MacGavran's and Spradley's ideas. Steve Hawthorne led the way in this. Much of the philosophy and method detailed in this manual was born in his visionary mind. Although he moved on from Caleb Project to another ministry in 1992, his influence is still felt throughout the fabric of Caleb Project Research.

Distinctive Characteristics

Six distinctives characterize Caleb Project Research – some make it more effective, others limit its effectiveness or scope.

An American Bias

Caleb Project Research has been born out of Western minds thinking in Western ways. Nearly all of the people who have had significant input into its development have been Americans. This has resulted in a system of research that works very well for Americans and often answers the questions they are asking. The method has not been employed by many non-Americans. However, a group of Koreans and Korean-Americans have adapted it to meet their needs. In the past this has been used by a bi-national team of Mexicans and Americans are using it to explore a city in Mexico. We can make no apologies for working within the context of our culture. However, we recognize that this approach cannot be adopted by people of other cultures without adjustments.

Another Code of Ethics

We also feel a need to be honest about our attitudes toward standard social science practices and ethics. With church planting as a key goal of our research, we trounce some of the most sacred ethical guidelines of modern anthropology: to observe, but not to change. In addition, our cultural helpers do not know that we use their information for the purpose of church planting. Revealing the intent of our research would most likely skew the information shared with us, or prevent cultural helpers from participating. Therefore, we explain our research apart from church planting goals. This is not acceptable by academic standards but we feel that we are operating according to another code of ethics. God desires for all men to know him, and he deserves praise from everyone. We do not force anyone to help with our research. As Christ's ambassadors, we seek to honor, respect, and bless each person we meet.

The Unreached: A Self-imposed Limitation

While our research method may be effective in many contexts, we have limited our work to unreached peoples in urban settings. As a result, most of our experience is in pioneer church-planting situations overseas. This has been a self-imposed limitation. Our method may well have great usefulness in other contexts. It may be used for spreading the gospel among people groups that already have a viable Christian witness in their midst. It may also be effective in rural settings or for work among unreached peoples living outside their homelands.

Priority: Mobilization

Caleb Project has also kept as its heart and soul a desire to mobilize Christians for the completion of the Great Commission. We view our research as a means to mobilize Christians. As we conduct research among a given people, our desire is for our team members, the American church, and missionaries to be informed and encouraged regarding God's plans for that people. Our mobilization goals consistently win out over our research goals. We understand that others may give research higher priority than we have. If this is the case, please adjust or supplement our method to meet your research needs.

Team Work

All of our experience with this research method has been in the context of short-term teams. While some of the implications of working as a team are presented in Part IV, one issue is important to consider here. All the people who have used our research method have been novices. They have been trained quickly, but in a short time on the field, they have done worthwhile research. You do not have to be an anthropology expert to put this method into action. A key reason that novices have been successful is that we have enabled them to work together as a team. Rather than sending a lone ethnographer to solo his or her way through a new culture, we have placed ten or so people together to build on one another's growing knowledge. This synergistic effect results in gathering a larger quantity of higher quality insight than any individual could accomplish in the same length of time.

Dependence on Prayer

We feel that the quality of our research is also enhanced by our dependence on prayer. Prayer permeates the life of Caleb Project Research Expeditions. Specifically, research teams spend each morning in corporate prayer. Then as they go through the day, research partners pray for each other and ask God to lead them to cultural helpers. They pray for these friends and for the establishment of a church in their city.

Teams also dedicate half a day each week to prayer for their city. On the appointed day, team members gather for an hour of worship. Then they disperse in pairs to various parts of the city and spend up to three hours walking through neighborhoods and commercial districts, praying as they go. Their basic model for prayer can be summed up as worship of God, warfare against evil, and welcoming Christ's kingdom. Following prayerwalks, team members gather together to report what they prayed and to share any insights they gained.

Team members' prayers make a difference for the gospel in their cities. Prayerwalks also lead to spiritual discernment and insight regarding the research. For further information on prayerwalks, we highly recommend *Prayerwalking: Praying On-Site With Insight* by Steve Hawthorne and Graham Kendrick.

Conclusion

Finally, you may be wondering about the results of this research. To date we have written strategy reports for more than twenty-five different church-planting situations. Numerous teams are employing them to choose a ministry focus, to determine how they will proceed and to solve the challenging problems they face after many years of ministry.

A church planter in South Asia, who is a Muslim convert, recently reported, "I have used Caleb Project's research throughout my work here. Their strategy reports are required reading for our new teams." This man will soon hand off the church he is planting to another national leader in order to begin anew elsewhere. he hopes a Caleb Project Research Expedition will precede him in his next locale, too.

A long-term church planter on his way to an unreached Middle Eastern city recently commented on our report for that city, "I have great enthusiasm to go, knowing the way has been prepared by prayer. We go depending on that prayer as well as depending on and utilizing Caleb Project's research. It's foundational to our strategy."

Our Manual Format

Exploring the Land has been arranged so that you can ingest relevant information in the shortest amount of time. Part I addresses the foundational beliefs and philosophy which guide our research. Caleb Project Research is more than a list of questions. Part I has not been included to provide window dressing. An understanding of this material is crucial to effectively implementing the research method. Part II presents the overall research process and the specific skills you will need to go out and engage in productive ethnographic research. Part III presents the basic categories of investigation that are used in Caleb Project Research. Part IV concludes with an example of an entire Caleb Project Research Expedition. Specific advice is provided for those who plan to work as a team to do research.

Appendices I, II, and III provide a brief introduction to Caleb Project, our resources, and our People Specific Advocate program. Appendix IV provides recruiting profiles for a research team. Many technical and foreign words are used throughout this manual. We have included a glossary with helpful definitions to aid your reading. Material provided in References can be used to locate resources we have utilized and to supplement this manual.

Part I: Building a Foundation

Four cornerstones form the foundation of Caleb Project Research. Our foundational belief deals with what we hold to be true about God, his purposes throughout history, and how he involves us in them. Our foundational assumptions serve as the missiological signposts guiding our response to God's commission. Our foundational questions are the three main questions we try to answer as we join in God's purposes. And our foundational perspective is the viewpoint from which we ask those questions. The areas of research interest that you will find in Part III take their structure and purpose from these principles.

Foundational Belief: God Gathers Followers From All Peoples

Believers throughout the ages have been concerned with certain fundamental questions regarding God and our relationship to him. From the thoughtful missionary to the successful businessman to the grieving parent, these fundamental cries are raised: What is God doing? What are his desires for me, for my family, for the world? What is God up to when we find ourselves prospering beyond our expectations? What is he about when we face uncertainty and despair which threatens to consume us? What does he have in mind for a world which seems to totter on the brink of collapse?

What is God doing? What are his desires for me, for my family, for the world?

If we take a step back from our circumstances and catch a panoramic view of God and history in the Bible, we begin to discern some of what God intends for the human race. Understanding that, we begin to see how we fit in.

From Genesis through the Psalms and Prophets, from Jesus' life and death through John's vision of eternity, we see God in pursuit of his wayward creation. In Genesis 3, we overhear God asking Adam, "Where are you?" Later in Genesis 12, God calls Abram, declaring that he will bless Abram and through him all families of the earth will be blessed. In Psalm 66 we see that God has done awesome works on man's behalf. The psalmist exhorts us, "Shout with joy to God, all the earth! Say to God, 'How awesome are your deeds!'" (Psalm 66:1, 3a).

Isaiah the prophet also writes about God's pursuit of man. "I summon you by name ... though you do not acknowledge me .... Turn to me and be saved all you ends of the earth; for I am God, and there is not other" (Isaiah 45:4b-c, 22).

... the even greater glory is that God is known.

Jesus' final instructions to his followers were to "make disciples of all nations." Jesus does not refer to political entities when he speaks of all nations. Rather, he uses the word *ethne* to charge his disciples to gather followers from all peoples. This harkens back to God's promise to Abram that all the families of the earth would be blessed through him.

In Revelation (see 5:9 and 7:9), at the consummation of history, John sees before the throne of God representatives from every tribe, tongue, people, and nation. What God determined to do since before time began, what we see him pursue throughout Scripture, has finally come to pass. He has gathered followers for himself from all the families of the earth. He has redeemed a remnant from among all peoples. To what end? Certainly to the end of the remnant's salvation. But beyond that, to the end that God is glorified in a cosmic chorus made up of the unique strains of each of the peoples he loves so dearly. Man is redeemed, but the even greater glory is that God is known. God is adored. God is lifted up in proper, deserved, and eternal glory.

So what is God up to? Our foundational belief is that God works to gather for himself followers from among every people on the earth. He does this that men might know him and be saved. He does this because he is love. He does this so that men might give him the glory he deserves.

An amazing footnote to this foundational belief is the fact that God chooses to use us in the process of achieving his goals. People are an essential part of God's plan to redeem and reign. Peter declares this wonder in chapter two, verse nine of his first letter, "But you are a chosen people, a royal priesthood, a holy nation, *a people belonging to God, that you may declare the praises of him* who called you out of darkness into his wonderful light."

Foundational Assumptions: Missiological Building Blocks

As we join with God to bring about a following for himself from among all peoples, we rest our work on five building blocks. These building blocks serve as the missiological assumptions of our research. They give us reason to do research. They serve as a starting point that directs us toward crucial questions to ask, and they help us to interpret and apply the data we collect.

Working to Finish

Assumption

The work of missions is not an endless saga. It is a part of history which God has set in motion and which God will consummate. We firmly believe that God has called the Church to join with him to gather a remnant from among all peoples and that at some point, as God determines, that task will be completed.

Biblical Basis

As far back as the fall in Genesis 3, God indicates that he will triumph. God promises that though the serpent will bruise the heel of the woman's seed, his head will be crushed in the process. In Romans 11:25 Paul speaks about an in-gathering of non-Jews preceding an awakening in Israel. Jesus, in Matthew 24:14, said that the gospel would be preached as a witness to all nations, then the end would come. These passages show God bringing history to a close.

Relevance

Believing that we are finishing an assignment causes us to direct our research efforts to the parts of the world with the least gospel presence. If the Church has been given the task of evangelizing the nations of the earth, then it is logical to apply effort to the areas and peoples as yet untouched.

The kingdom of God expands primarily through spiritual work carried out by God.

This assumption also provides a basis for hope that God will establish his church even in places where it has long been absent. God would not give a mandate without a definite plan to complete it – maybe in our generation, maybe a thousand years from now, but destined to be completed.

Ministry is Warfare

Assumption

The kingdom of God expands primarily through spiritual work carried out by God. We believe that God calls us to apply our minds to the work of the kingdom, but that mental effort is secondary to spiritual force in the transfer of men's souls from darkness to light.

Biblical Basis

In Matthew 22:37, Jesus quotes Deuteronomy 6:5 in response to a question about the greatest commandment. He tells the inquirer, "You shall love the Lord your God with all your heart, and with all your soul, and with all your mind" (NASB). So our minds have a place in our efforts to love and serve God. But Paul reminds us in Ephesians 6:12 that, "... our struggle is not against flesh and blood, but against ... spiritual forces of wickedness in the heavenly places" (NASB). Paul also says in 2 Corinthians 10:4 "... the weapons of our warfare are not of the flesh, but divinely powerful for the destruction of fortresses" (NASB).

Relevance

In light of this, we apply our minds with all diligence to the problem of church-lessness among many peoples. Even so, we recognize that our strategizing and problem solving are secondary to the spiritual work that must take place. Therefore, Caleb Project research teams spend significant time in prayer and worship, exalting God in their city. Through prayer they attempt to discern God's plans for the city, as well as Satan's hindrances to those plans.

Primacy of Churches

Assumption

Since the time of Jesus, the local church has been the foundational unit in the advance of the kingdom of God. In other words, God's primary agent of redemption is the church.

Biblical Basis

The local church serves as the underlying context for almost every line of the New Testament. While little space is given to describe specifically what the church should look like, the whole book assumes local churches to be the operative unit of the kingdom of God.

Relevance

This assumption compels us in our research to look beyond the dissemination of the gospel message, beyond the conversion of individuals, and beyond discipleship to the establishment of reproducing churches. While we expect our research to shed light on appropriate gospel proclamation and on evangelism and discipleship, we focus that light on the local churches we desire to see planted.

This assumption also leads us to focus on church planting strategies rather than on social development ministries. While the latter are important and certainly part of God's work, we believe that social change is affected most significantly and lastingly through the redeeming presence and work of indigenous local churches.

A Church for Every People

Assumption

God plans to establish his Church among every people. We further believe that manifestations of the Church will be unique for each people.

What is a People Group?

A helpful article on the topic of people group definition can be found in the Vol. 7 No. 2 April 1990 issue of the International Journal of Frontier Missions. *The article was written by Patrick Johnstone and is entitled "People Groups: How Many are Unreached." Because our research is done primarily in English, our focus in thinking about people groups has necessarily been on sociological distinctives rather than on ethnolinguistic distinctives. A great overlap exists between the two, and we do not ignore ethnolinguistic factors. These factors can be understood to a high degree through sociological* realities.

Biblical Basis

In Genesis 12:3, God promised that through Abraham *all* the families of the earth would be blessed. Jesus commissioned his disciples in Matthew 28:19 to make disciples of *all* nations. John sees in Revelation 7:9, "... a great multitude ... from *every* nation, and *all* tribes and peoples and tongues, standing before the throne and before the Lamb" (NASB).

Relevance

Building upon the assumption that the local church is God's primary agent of redemption, and with a mind to finish the task of world evangelization, we quickly face this question: How many churches are enough? Today churches exist in most, if not all, countries of the earth. Is this sufficient? If a church is planted in every country, would the task of making disciples of all nations be completed?

Biblical references to "nations" and "Gentiles" usually refer to what we would call ethnic groups. In the Great Commission, Jesus instructs his followers to go and make disciples of all nations, essentially, of all ethnicities, all people groups. He uses the same term in Matthew 24:14 when he says that, "for this gospel of the kingdom shall be preached in the whole world for a witness to all the *nations*, and then the end shall come" (NASB). We believe, therefore, that the task is completed when God has established a reproducing church among all people groups.

This logic, of course, turns on the definition of a people group. While different definitions abound, for our research we will define a people group as the largest group of people within which the gospel can spread as a church-planting movement without encountering barriers of acceptance and understanding. So a church planted in each people group would fulfill the Great Commission.

The assumption of a church for every people also addresses our belief that the church should, and naturally will, grow up in ways unique to each people. Among other things, this uniqueness will likely be expressed through language, worship and leadership styles, and evangelism and discipleship patterns. Such unique-to-the-people churches are important on two levels.

First, they are important to God's glory. God has created unique cultures and desires to receive unique praise from each culture. God speaks throughout the Bible about gathering a following from all peoples. We believe he desires this not so that he has a complete set, one of every color, like a full box of

crayons. Rather, each people group has a unique way to express God's praise, a praise that will only be complete when some from every tribe and tongue are expressing it.

God has created unique cultures and desires to receive unique praise from each culture.

Second, we have reason to believe that people find it easier to become part of a fellowship that is culturally their own. Particularly in pioneer situations, we want to use the natural affinity people have for others who think and look and talk like they do. We do not, however, intend to reinforce or encourage prejudice of any kind. Such prejudice in the church would disregard the unity believers ought to share – having one body, and one Lord over all (see Ephesians 4:1-6).

Working Together

Assumption

God uses all parts of the body of Christ, as he determines, to accomplish the work of missions. North Americans alone have not been entrusted to take the gospel to the ends of the earth. Neither, however, have they been disqualified or displaced by third world missionaries or national workers. All who claim the name of Christ are working under his headship to accomplish his plans.

Biblical Basis

Paul talks extensively in favor of working together as a body and in opposition to factions among believers (see Ephesians 2:8-22 and Philippians 2:1-4).

Relevance

We must consider how God desires for believers from all nations to serve as his ambassadors among the peoples we research. No particular field belongs to one mission agency or to representatives of a certain nationality. North Americans may need more than others to grow in grace and humility, but all who rally to

Christ's banner need to work in partnership with each other under submission to our common Head.

Stating the Problem: The Barriers We Face

Caleb Project Research is essentially a problem solving endeavor. The problem is that a majority of humankind is out of relationship with God. People live lives of desperation and die to spend eternity apart from God. That in itself is tragic. Moreover, God is denied the praise and honor he deserves from those persons. Beyond individuals, this dynamic is at work in whole populations, entire people groups within which there is no church. This is the essence of the problem we have set our hearts and minds to solving.

With this premise in mind, a logical starting point would be to ask, "Why aren't people following God?" This question could quickly take us into a discussion of the relationship of God's sovereignty to man's free will, a puzzle that has perplexed and divided theologians throughout Christian history. May it suffice to say here that God is sovereign and he must do something for people to be able to follow him in Christ. Somehow in his plan, however, God calls believers to involvement. We are witnesses and ambassadors, junior partners in the work of redemption. As such, the quality of our witness can vary. We should strive to be the best we can in these roles, realizing that God alone provides all grace and wisdom – literally everything – needed for men and women to follow him.

Perhaps everything standing in the way of people following God can be contained in two categories: barriers of understanding and barriers of acceptance. People either do not understand the gospel, so they cannot follow, or lack understanding, so they choose not to accept it.

Barriers of Understanding

Why aren't people following God?

In many cases people do not follow God because they have not heard the gospel. In *Our Globe and How to Reach It,* David Barrett and Todd Johnson assert that some 1.3 billion people in 12,000 people groups have not heard the gospel. Paul asks in Romans 10:14b, "And how can they believe in the one of whom they have not heard? And how can they hear without someone preaching to them?"

We can logically assume from this that some of these 1.3 billion people would follow Christ if they were to hear of him. So we find ourselves harvesting little, because, at least in part, we have sown little. Some people don't understand because they have not been told.

But can we assume that everyone who is told about the gospel actually understands it? In some situations the gospel may be spoken loudly, but not clearly. Consider the story of Cameron Townsend, the man who founded Wycliffe Bible Translators. After Townsend arrived in Guatemala in 1917, he was tramping around the villages, handing out Spanish-language scriptures. In one village, an Indian who did not read Spanish approached him and asked, "If your God is so great, why doesn't he speak in my language?" This startling question confirmed Townsend's doubts regarding the efficacy of Spanish evangelism for Guatemala's Indians. It also eventually led Townsend to form Wycliffe Bible Translators and to spend fifty years advocating the translation of the Bible into all heart languages. (See *www.wycliffe.org/history/WBT* for full story).

This illustrates one way in which the gospel may be preached, but not really heard. When the heart language is not used, the gospel is not preached in a way which really communicates. Converts rarely result.

A more subtle example of failure to effectively communicate can be seen in the early efforts of Campus Crusade for Christ in Thailand. Young Crusaders using the Four Spiritual Laws booklet found themselves surprisingly unsuccessful. Upon investigation, they came to understand that the absence of a deity in the Buddhist cosmology rendered unintelligible the first law ("God loves you and has a wonderful plan for your life."). Thai students would ask, if only in their minds, "What is god?" Campus Crusade responded to this by printing an evangelistic tool specifically for Thais. This new booklet included a brief explanation of an uncreated Creator. The gospel was more clearly communicated, and more Thai students began following Christ.

When there is a lack of understanding, we must be particularly careful that our message makes its way into the hearts of listeners. This is known, in mission circles, as contextualization. For example, Peter's message to the Jews in Acts 2 differed considerably in style and approach from Paul's message to the Athenian Greeks in Acts 17. Likewise, our message to a tribal group in the Amazon, while thoroughly biblical, would differ from our equally biblical message to Berbers in Morocco. We would adapt the message to the context in which it was spoken.

In response to barriers of understanding we generally turn our attention to the missionary's message: the language, dialect, idiom, and illustrations a missionary uses, the role he plays in society, the clothes he wears, or where he sets up residence.

These are important issues to consider. And they are the most natural to consider given the tendency of human nature to focus our attention on ourselves. As a result, nearly all missions research seeks to conquer barriers of understanding by improving communication. Great advances have followed. Yet we are still faced with a world in which the church has yet to gain a foothold in some 12,000 people groups. Certainly the gospel must be preached, and it must be communicated to specific peoples in unique and understandable ways. But is that all that is necessary?

Beyond barriers of understanding, another entire set of barriers keep people from following Christ. Many who have heard and understood the message fail to follow because they are unable to accept the message. Others who have never heard may also encounter barriers of acceptance when church-planting efforts eventually begin among them. Such peoples are often labeled unreceptive or resistant. Some people groups certainly are. But if we stop with that explanation, we risk oversimplifying the situation. Barriers of acceptance are multifaceted and complex, but God can give us understanding to overcome many of them.

Barriers of Acceptance

Offense of the Cross

As we see in the Bible and have likely seen in our own lives, some people will not follow Christ because of the offense inherent in the gospel. 1 Corinthians 1:18 says, "For the word of the cross is to those who are perishing foolishness, but to us who are being saved it is the power of God" (NASB). Because of pride and disbelief, some people refuse to follow Christ. To do so we must accept that we cannot face life and death on our own, that we are sinners who need a savior. People often resist this truth.

Christianity is "Western"

Sometimes people do not accept the gospel they have heard and understood because they perceive the faith to be foreign. In many cities where Caleb Project teams have conducted research, we have heard, "To be a Turk (or Malay, Kazakh, Bohra, etc.) is to be Muslim." Thai people have told us, "Christianity is for the white man, Buddhism is for the Thai." People may understand the basics of the gospel message but honestly believe that it is not for them. Until believers can explain or demonstrate the transcultural nature of the gospel, potential converts may not even listen.

Following Christ = Denying Culture

Sometimes we find people refusing to accept Christ due to an inflated perception of what following him entails. No biblical Christian would deny that there is a cost to following Christ, but for some the perception of that cost is blown out of proportion. For example, in Bombay, Muslims make up 15 percent of the 10 million inhabitants of the city. Their primary exposure to the gospel comes from Catholic believers in the city. The perception of many Muslims is that to follow Christ, they must leave their community and join the Catholic community. In their minds, this would involve things which are grievous to them, such as leaving their families, and things which are anathema, such as eating pork, drinking alcohol, and worshiping idols.

Pioneering is Tough

Finally, we must remember that in pioneer situations, the first believers begin to follow Christ with no precedent. No church made up of people who speak their language and share their culture exists. Like Neil Armstrong stepping onto the moon, they drop their first footsteps where no one like them has walked. Who among us would have the courage to accept Christ if that were true for us?

The Church's response to barriers of acceptance should be like Jesus' interaction with the woman at the well. In John 4, we see Christ addressing cultural barriers in his efforts to evangelize the Samaritan adulteress. She believes Jesus expects her to become a Jew in order to be acceptable to God. Jesus tells her that God is not looking for Samaritans who will become Jews, but rather people who will worship him in spirit and in truth. When the disciples return from their food foray into a nearby town, they are shocked to see Jesus finishing a conversation with a Samaritan woman and drinking the water she has offered him. As she scurries back to town, Jesus refuses the disciples' offer of food and explains to them that his food is to do the work of God. He then tells them, perhaps as he points to a crowd coming down the road toward them from the village, that the fields are white for harvest. John goes on to say that Jesus stayed for two days in that village and many believed.

The Muslims of Bombay

"There are one and a half million Muslims in Bombay ... and only a handful of persecuted, scattered converts. No church has yet been effective in reaching out to them," explained a leading national Christian. Churches in Bombay are filled with Catholics and converted Hindus, but devoid of converted Muslims. Since the Muslims invaded India 800 years ago, the situation has remained the same. No generation of Muslims has yet been reached with the gospel. The need for compassionate, committed Christians to live and share the good news with Bombay Muslims is great.

The disciples quickly assumed that the Samaritans were not qualified candidates for God's kingdom. Jesus, on the other hand, removed the barriers that kept the woman, and in turn the villagers, from accepting the good news for themselves. Like the disciples, we too need to reconsider whether peoples must renounce their culture to follow Christ. Perhaps needless barriers of acceptance hinder them from doing so.

To cross barriers of understanding, we must change how a missionary communicates. By contrast, to cross barriers of acceptance, we must focus on the on the people themselves, seeking to understand who they are and what an indigenous church would look like for them. In this way, needless barriers of acceptance can be eliminated.

While both sets of barriers must be addressed, Caleb Project Research tends to focus on barriers of acceptance. We believe that many of the important questions in this area can be understood by short-term missionaries researching in English. Communication barriers, on the other hand, often require a full understanding of the language and a seasoned perspective on contextualization.

Foundational Questions

Our emphasis on barriers of acceptance leads us to ask three fundamental research questions: Who are the peoples? What are they like? And, how can they be reached with the gospel? Let us consider these questions in greater depth.

"Who Are the Peoples?"

The librarian leaned over his desk so that his face was only inches from mine. In a soft voice, which I felt as well as heard, he confessed, "No, the Bohras would never come to this mosque. They have their own. And we would never allow our daughters to marry them." This insight came five minutes into an interview in the Islamic library of a large Indian mosque. I had begun by asking what different kinds of Muslims lived in the city. Our friend had rocked back in his chair, bobbed his head in a distinctly Indian way and assured my me, "Oh, Muslims are all 'same same.' We are brothers. There are no divisions."

If a missionary desiring to plant churches in this Indian city accepted the librarian's first statement he might find great difficulty in bringing a church to life. People group divisions *do* exist among India's Muslims. An odd assortment of new converts from different Muslim communities would resist forming a fellowship in the same way that poles on a magnet resist coming together. People more naturally form allegiances with others who they consider "us" while repelling those they consider "them." People group divisions, while rarely more distinct and visible than in India, are powerful wherever they are found. A primary pursuit of Caleb Project Research is the discernment of "us" and "them" distinctions in a given collection of people. The research question that corresponds to this pursuit is "Who are the peoples?"

Three things that we do not intend to do should be noted here. We do not want to lay a preconceived segmentation on the people. Rather than slicing an apple into identical pieces, we are peeling a tangerine to see how it falls apart on its own. Secondly, we are not trying to enumerate the highest possible number of groups. Believing that each people group by definition requires a separate church-planting effort, we rejoice in finding fewer, rather than more, groups. Finally, we are not promoting prejudice. We do not believe that redeemed people should continue to shun others due to ethnic distinctions, past grievances, or anything else. Cultural distinctiveness does not absolve churches from seeking meaningful unity with one another.

"What Are They Like?"

The second research question, "What are they like?" helps us discover everything about a people group that is relevant to the establishment of culturally appropriate churches among them. We want to understand how members of a people group relate to others. We also want to understand the forces which affect the social evolution of a particular people group. For example, how do families work? What role does religion play in their lives? What do they hope and dream for? How do

A primary pursuit of Caleb Project Research is the discernment of "us" and "them" distinctions in a given collection of people.

What Are Village Uzbeks Like?

In a village just ten miles from Samarkand, Uzbekistan, Dilia prepares dough for Uzbek bread. For Uzbeks, bread carries deep, life-giving significance and is a vital part of many Uzbek national traditions.

Dilia and most of her family work on a collective farm, the economic foundation of the village. Her 65-year-old mother-in-law cares for the children, while Dilia works in the fields from sunup to sundown. Other family members regularly commute to the city for school, factory jobs, prayer at the mosque, and shopping in the market.

Toxic pesticides, bad water and poor hygiene make life difficult in Uzbek villages. Few people with university training want to move to the village to teach or to practice medicine, thus perpetuating low standards. City dwellers consider villagers poor and uneducated. Most villagers, however, prefer their large homes and gardens as well as the sense of community they share in their rural setting.

Since the young consider religion uninteresting, only the elderly take time for the practice of Islam. Old men attend Friday prayers at the mosque or discuss religion in tea houses, called choikhonas.

About 75% of Uzbeks in Uzbekistan live in villages, which are often interconnected by extended family networks. If a culturally relevant church were planted in one village, the gospel could spread to other villages through family ties.

they perceive their history? The more we know about a people group, the more we are able to envision what the church might look like for that group.

"How Can They Be Reached?"

The third primary question that Caleb Project Research seeks to answer is how an unreached people can find God's way for them to follow Christ. Essentially, how can they be reached? This question helps us understand what kind of church we desire to plant.

Two realities guide us as we consider what the church might look like for a particular people group: biblical authenticity and cultural acceptability. The church within its culture must be completely subject to the guidance and parameters of the Bible. While the Bible is the first and final authority for the shape of the church in any culture, many aspects of the church are not rigidly outlined. God has given leeway for churches to flourish in unique ways within each culture.

Understanding various aspects of the culture helps us envision churches which, while biblically authentic, are also relevant to the culture. Such a contextualized church is beneficial both to God and to the people among whom it is born. God receives the unique glory he deserves from the people, and barriers are broken down so that more and more from the group may follow Christ.

Foundational Perspective: Envisioning

In his bestselling book, *The Seven Habits of Highly Effective People*, Steven Covey talks about a habit he calls beginning with the end in mind.

> *To begin with the end in mind means to start with a clear understanding of your destination. It means to know where you're going so that you better understand where you are now and so that the steps you take are always in the right direction .... If the ladder [we are climbing] is not leaning against the right wall, every step we take just gets us to the wrong place faster. We may be very busy, we may be very efficient, but we will also be truly effective only when we begin with the end in mind* (page 98).

Beginning with the end in mind, which we call "envisioning," serves as the final support structure in the foundation of Caleb Project Research. It is the *perspective* with which we view the development of church-planting strategy. But it is also an *activity*. We want to begin church-planting work with a good idea of the church movement we desire to result from our work. If we want to begin with the end in mind, we need to figure out, however vaguely, what the end looks like. Only then can we have it in mind. This process of figuring out the end, we call "envisioning." Perhaps it should be called "end-visioning."

Envisioning as a Perspective

As a perspective, envisioning focuses more on end results than on current activity. That is not to say that the end justifies the means. Rather, we first determine *where* we want to go, *then* how to get there. For many people this is a new way to approach church planting. By nature, our tendency is to begin from where we are, and step by step, move out. Envisioning, however, urges us to consider first where we want to go, then tailor each step so that, as best as we can tell, our efforts take us to our desired end.

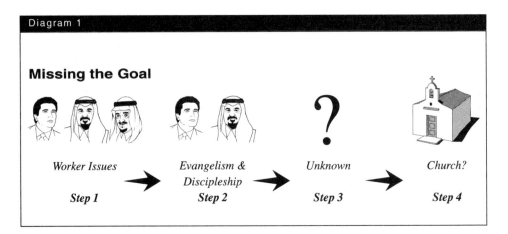

Diagram 1

Missing the Goal

Worker Issues	Evangelism & Discipleship	Unknown	Church?
Step 1	Step 2	Step 3	Step 4

Diagrams 1 and 2 illustrate two different approaches to church planting. Diagram 1, Missing the Goal, shows how we might naturally approach church planting in a pioneer situation. In Step 1 we would figure out how to gain access to our target people, master a language to communicate with them, and then assume a suitable role in society. Our attention would move to the next step of building relationships, witnessing to people, and sharing our faith. After a person converts, we would disciple them, helping them grow up in the faith. After several had converted, we might attempt to form a church. Two possibilities confront us here. The new church may reflect what we have known within our own culture, regardless of that model's relevance to the people we are working among. Or, we may get stuck having no real ideas about what the church should look like (see Step 3: Unknown).

Granted, if we pursue the model presented in Diagram 1, during the early stages we would gain insight that could help us understand what a church for a particular people group might look like. Consider, though, how much more effective the second model could be (see Diagram 2, Beginning With the End in Mind). In this model, great thought and prayer is given to understanding what the church might look like (the activity of envisioning) *before* we begin. The picture we have of the resulting church helps us determine what life after conversion might look like. In turn, life after conversion would determine what our evangelism and discipleship should look like. Finally, our evangelism and discipleship give insight into what language we should learn, how to get into relationships with appropriate people, and how to remain among our target group. This perspective of beginning with the end in mind – working backward before going forward – is envisioning.

Envisioning as an Activity

To begin with the end in mind and work accordingly, we must have some tangible idea of what the end is. Our church planting goal is the establishment of indigenous, multiplying churches. Envisioning helps us articulate ideas about the distinct manifestations of the church while we are learning about our target people group. We want to catch a glimpse of God's future for an unreached within their own culture. Envisioning is projecting carefully, almost timidly, what evangelization might look like for the people we are learning about. Researchers ask, "What does God want for these people? What are his dreams for them? What would this city look like if the gospel were to bloom and flourish here?" Asking such lofty questions in a city of millions of unsaved people can overwhelm even a stout heart with despair. Therefore, envisioning requires hope. That hope must be seated firmly in the realization that God has promised to do something among all people – that he is more than able, and often does things we can hardly believe. He is more concerned with and committed to the glorification of his name than we are.

Envisioning can be understood by dissecting this definition:

> *Envisioning is the development of a biblically based, research informed, prayer saturated hypothesis about what an indigenous church might look like within an unreached people group.*

Development

Understanding what the church might look like in a pioneer situation is not an activity to be accomplished at once. Our understanding of the church grows in accordance with our understanding of the culture. A picture of the resulting church develops over time, so we must hold with open hands what we believe the church will look like. It is appropriate that we have ideas, but also that we accept their refinement or disposal.

Biblically based

The Bible, not culture, must be the first source guiding our church planting in pioneer situations. While we may be tempted to over-adapt in order to see the church gain a foothold in a new area, we must not compromise Scripture.

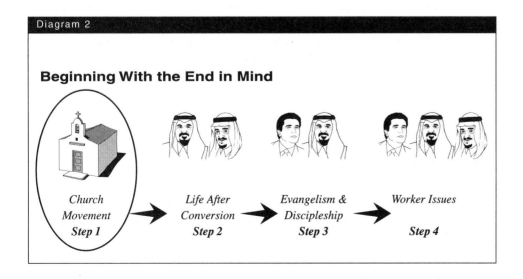

Diagram 2

Beginning With the End in Mind

Church Movement — **Step 1**

Life After Conversion — **Step 2**

Evangelism & Discipleship — **Step 3**

Worker Issues — **Step 4**

Research informed

We research to understand the culture so that we can envision what the church will look like, that is, how people can find ways to follow Christ that fit them culturally. We look into the history of the people to see what inroads the gospel may have made in the past and what has resulted. The successes and failures of those who have gone before can serve as signposts to guide our work.

Prayer saturated

All research and envisioning must be saturated in prayer. Our wisdom, even our understanding of the Bible, falls far short of what the day requires.
God must move on our behalf if we are to understand anything about his desires for the people we are researching. God has promised to pour out wisdom without reproach on those who ask him.

Hypothesis

When all is said and done, our research leaves us with a guess – albeit an educated one, but a guess nonetheless – about what the church might look like for the people we have researched. We do not presume to see the future, and we refuse to insist that our vision be brought to reality. What we do end up with, however, is a good idea and a goal to shoot for.

Indigenous

The church that we long to see established among the people we research should be wholly theirs. God will unveil their way to worship and exalt him and to live under his lordship. This is pleasing to God, who has pledged to ransom a remnant from among all people. We also believe such a culturally relevant church will maintain a strong foothold in pioneer situations.

Dangers of Envisioning

Working hard to understand where we want to end up before we begin will help improve our church-planting efforts. Even so, or perhaps because of this, the envisioning road is peppered with potholes that threaten to swallow the inattentive church planter. Satan will certainly contest our efforts to be used by God to establish his kingdom among unreached peoples. There are at least three dangers inherent in envisioning.

Only My Way

When we invest considerable energy in researching a people group and envisioning the church in their midst, we can become very protective of our vision. We decide for our own ministry or impose on others a single recipe which, if followed precisely, will result in an indigenous, multiplying church.

Such a demand for our plan goes against the spirit of hopeful dreaming that envisioning represents. It also overestimates our ability to see what the church might look like before we begin work. Most dangerously, it takes the reins away from God. We must never forget that he may do something totally different from what we expect.

Non-biblical contextualization

Cultural knowledge can sidetrack our envisioning. We can become enamored of the culture and lose sight of the ways in which it is decidedly ungodly. In our eagerness to see people follow God we may compromise Scripture. We envision a church that is culturally relevant, but not biblically sound.

Table 1

Building A Foundation	
Foundational Belief	• *God Gathers Followers From All Peoples*
Foundational Assumptions	• *Working to Finish* • *Ministry is Warfare* • *Primacy of Churches* • *A Church for Every People* • *Working Together*
Foundational Questions	• *Who Are the Peoples?* • *What Are They Like?* • *How Can They Be Reached?*
Foundational Perspective	• *Envisioning: Beginning With the End in Mind*

Despair

In a strategy meeting for an Indian city, a dejected researcher despaired, "The church has not been planted here in 800 years! Who do we think *we* are?" The reality of lost peoples with histories empty of gospel witness can be shattering. Satan would love for us to throw our hands up in surrender and to despair at what we see. The greater reality however, is that God's promises are true. A remnant from every people *will* raise their hands in worship to him. We can look forward with sober, but unquenchable faith that God will honor his promise. Indeed, over time, God gave that researcher and his team hope for their city. Today a small Muslim convert fellowship meets there. God will not be stopped.

Part II: Getting Ready

Introduction

In Part I, we have built a foundation and put a framework for research in place. Essentially, we want to see God worshiped where he is not. We believe that he is at work to bring some from all nations into his kingdom. He is building his Church and even the gates of hell will not prevail against it (see Matthew 16:18).

Our particular approach to the problem of 1.3 billion unreached people is to enter their cities as learners. As we do so, we stand on a strong biblical foundation, on a particular understanding of people groups, and on a firm belief in the value of mobilization. From the perspective of mobilization, we do research in order to use it. We want our research to be presented in ways that inform and shape Christians' response to the unreached.

From the perspective of cultural learning, we want to understand and describe people groups and the cities in which they live. Our research efforts are aimed broadly at answering the questions "Who are the peoples?" "What are they like?" and "How can they be reached?" In doing so, we hope to offer insights for current or future Christian workers as they labor to plant churches. Finally, the entire perspective from which we view our work can be stated as "beginning with the end in mind." Now that we have provided this backdrop for your work, you can get ready for field research among unreached peoples. Part II introduces each ethnographic skill you will need to carry out an entire research project – from designing your project to writing a final report.

Research Design

The first step in getting ready for a research project is to design it. What will you research? How will you do it? What goals do you hope to achieve? Our research design includes two essential elements: fieldwork and teamwork. Some cultural learning can be done in the library, by meeting international students, or by talking to others who have lived and worked overseas. Some information can also be gathered on short, fact-finding trips. But to adequately address the three over-arching research questions of "Who are the peoples?" "What are they like?" and "How can they be reached?" we feel that it is necessary to go and live among the people and pursue relationship with them – to do fieldwork.

Second, our research design hinges on the multiplied effectiveness of team work. Each Caleb Project research team usually consists of 7-12 members who receive training in missiology and ethnography. Most of the training an individual researcher receives is presented in Parts II and III of this manual. Further details for those who desire to research as a team are included in Part IV.

Caleb Project researchers are committed to working together to carry out an extensive cultural study. They spend three months conducting full-time field work in a chosen urban setting. A few team members write and produce useful tools as products of the research after they return to the United States. Though we have always conducted this research in a team setting, we believe that our research method can certainly be adapted for individual use.

Whether you use a team or not, you must make choices about who will do the research, how researchers will be trained, where they will carry out research, and how long they will study overseas. Once these choices are made, the next step in getting ready is to develop your own research focus.

Developing a Research Focus

Begin developing your research focus even before going overseas. Do you want to investigate an entire city, or a particular people group living there? You need to network with people who have an interest in what you are doing and read what has already been written about a city or people group.

Networking

Investing time and effort in networking with missionaries, national workers, churches, and mission agencies can help in developing a useful research focus. These people have experience and wisdom to share about particular cities and people groups. In addition, time spent with these people builds trust and rapport – creating an open audience for your research findings.

For example, when we were first planning to send a research team to the newly opened Muslim republics of the former Soviet Union, we learned that one Christian man had been living there for three years as a scholar. After making a few phone calls, we found that he would soon visit the United States. When he arrived, we called to introduce ourselves and explained our desire to do research. This man gladly shared some of the cultural questions that were on his mind regarding Christian work among a particular people group. For instance, a pressing question on his mind was whether the very traditional people in his city might need a special ministry focus – he felt separated from them by nature of his work in a university setting. A research focus for our team became whether or not there might be people group distinctions between the traditional and the modern. This man also had relationships with other individuals who were interested in Central Asia, as well as with churches who faithfully prayed for this people group. Quickly, our network grew and we gained insight from each contact. Even a little networking begins the process of developing a research focus.

Building trust with people who have a vested interest in your research is also important. When we were planning to send a research team to an Arab country in the Middle East, we first contacted Christian leaders there. We asked for advice concerning our endeavor and about the need for research. Some leaders were interested in what we could learn but were concerned about overt connections between them and us, particularly while we were conducting studies. Their well-founded concerns rose from security situations they faced in Muslim lands. During an advance planning trip, we visited face-to-face with many of these leaders. Those meetings yielded a great reward. We learned many things about people in our target city. The leaders also realized that we were thoughtful and prayerful about what we wanted to do. Once they trusted us to follow their advice regarding security, they opened themselves to further consider our research findings.

Pre-Reading

Christians and secular academicians have often already written about particular countries, people groups, or cities. The data actually available in our information age can be overwhelming. Don't allow mounds of related information to keep you from reading as much as you can. Once, when we were preparing to send two research teams to Kazakhstan, we found two very valuable documents about the Kazakhs. One book described the history of the people so well that we felt how important the themes of repeated oppression and betrayal might be to this people's acceptance of the gospel. By interviewing cultural helpers with this information in mind, we were able to confirm, broaden, and powerfully illustrate this dynamic as it exists among the Kazakh people. Another book introduced the tribal nature of the Kazakh nation. This information helped the team to focus on whether barriers to the gospel might exist between different Kazakh tribes.

Taking the Scare Out of Research

What do you think of when you hear the word research? Some people think of white lab coats and test tubes, while others think of clipboards and questionnaires.

Learn by living, working, eating, talking, and playing with people.

But neither vision is accurate or useful for the kind of research you will do among unreached peoples. Using a few ethnographic tools, you can rather learn by living, working, eating, talking, and playing with people.

The friends you make will be your primary source of information about their people, their city, and their culture. But how will you meet them? What should you ask? How can you keep track of everything? At some point, the lofty goals we have introduced must be pursued through practical means. You will need certain skills to be successful. Some skills are broad – like how to think about such an undertaking. Other skills are specific – like basic language learning, participant observation, finding cultural helpers, interviewing, notetaking, applying research findings, and writing a final report. The remainder of Part II will focus on the use of these skills. Then, in Part III, we will step back to look at the particular topics of interest we have used in our research. Depending on your learning preference, you may skip to Part III after the section on interviewing, and then come back to Part II to finish reading about notetaking, applying research findings, and writing a report.

Three Thinking Skills and the FOQUS Cycle

Three broad thinking skills are needed for this type of research. They are the ability to form a theory, to clarify ideas, and to suggest a research method. To form a theory one must identify missiological problems and then suggest potential solutions to those problems. For example, you may face the problem of beginning an effective ministry in a new city or among a specific unreached people group. As a missionary having just finished language training, you may have a theory that your strategy for beginning a church-planting ministry should be for a team to live in a particular neighborhood and provide medical care.

The second skill, clarifying ideas, is the ability to articulate the ideas on which your theory is based. Let's build a little more on the example we have begun. Let's say that the reasons behind your ministry strategy are: (1) Team: You have been ineffective so far as a solo missionary. One reason has been your necessary focus on language learning. But you also see that you need other skilled workers to join you. (2) Location: The people you hope to target live in particular neighborhoods in the city. One of those neighborhoods seems to be a place where you could have daily contact with the people. A building there is also available for rent. And (3) Program: Medical ministry seems to be a greater, more urgent need than say, teaching English. Your wife is a nurse, and you know a medical technologist that you could recruit to join your team.

A third thinking skill is the ability to develop a research method. To develop a research method is to find a way to gather the information you need to test your ideas and form more accurate ones. A handy acronym to guide your use of these three thinking skills is FOQUS. We pronounce this acronym (**foh**-koos) to distinguish our learning cycle from other uses of the word "focus."

F	Focus and Fix goals
O	Observe
Q	Question
U	Understand and
S	Strategize

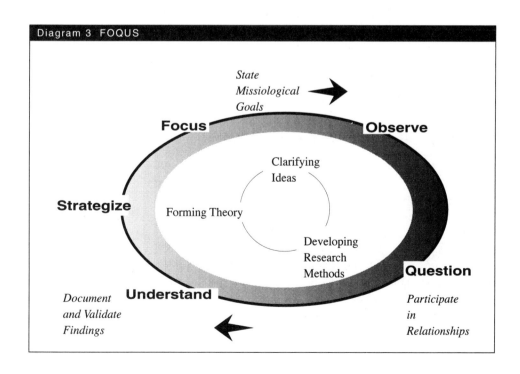

Diagram 3 FOQUS

FOQUS is a learning and thinking cycle that is used over and over again. The cycle incorporates all three aspects of thinking: forming theory, clarifying ideas, and developing a research method. You can use the FOQUS cycle repeatedly on a daily, weekly, or monthly basis to guide your entire learning experience. Using the illustration we have begun, you might use FOQUS in this way:

F   **Focus** on investigating neighborhoods. What makes one neighborhood a better place to begin ministry than another?

O   Sit along a main street in three different neighborhoods and **observe** the activities during different times of the day.

Q   Ask **questions** of at least three key members of each neighborhood – perhaps two prominent shop keepers and the head of a household. Good beginning questions might be "Please tell me about this neighborhood – what is it like?" More specific questions might be "Who lives in this neighborhood? How often do people from other parts of the city come here? Are there medical facilities here, or nearby? What are some difficulties that you face by locating your business in this part of town?"

U   **Understand** the real issues involved in the location of a new ministry. Write down what you learn from cultural helpers and make notes regarding the issues that come to light. Writing will clarify your ideas and help you know what to research next.

S   Make applications of cultural knowledge to the work of church planting. If needed, make a plan for further investigation. This is **strategizing** – using what you learn to make informed ministry decisions.

The FOQUS cycle can be used on a weekly and monthly basis as well. Form preliminary research goals that you or your team pursue for a length of time. After observing and asking questions, step back to strategize. If you need, conclude by writing about your findings.

Focus Your Goals for Research

A large part of your work is identifying and describing missiological issues. It is essential that you address areas that are missiologically significant. In other words, spend time learning about things that *really apply* to the work you hope to do, or are doing, among an unreached people group.

You can use a front door or back door approach to focus your goals for research. The front door approach is to decide from the outset which missiological problems you wish to investigate and then to devise a way to get insight into those problems (see Table 2). In a general sense, we have already provided broad research goals that constitute a front door approach. These goals are: Who are the peoples? What are they like? How can they be reached? In Part III, more specific areas of interest will be introduced. We believe that pursuing these questions will yield great insights for effective church planting.

The back door approach to research lacks a specific missiological problem (see Table 3 on the next page). Rather, a cultural discovery or hunch creeps up on you and you begin to discern that your ideas may have significant application to the task of church planting. The back door approach to research takes such a hunch and turns it into a specific plan for further learning.

Table 2 The Front Door Approach

State the missiological problem

We want to plant growing, indigenous churches that have strong, biblical leaders among traditional Turkmen.

State your theory

Growing, indigenous churches should be led by men who exercise leadership in ways that are common to Turkmen.

Clarify your ideas

Turkmen men, rather than women, seem to lead groups. How significant is this? What does it mean as we envision a church among traditional Turkmen?

Research objectives

*   Identify and describe leaders among traditional Turkmen. What are they like?

*   Collect ideas about style of leadership that Turkmen hold.

*   Catalogue community and family decisions that involve male leaders.

Table 3 The Back Door Approach

Cultural discovery

After talking with ten different cultural helpers (two are Kurds and eight are Turks) you have heard repeatedly that Turks and Kurds do not trust each other. They live in different areas within the city and have different occupations. For example, Turkish women are rarely found weaving bags and blankets but many Kurdish women make a living selling their weavings to tourists.

Possible significance

Perhaps a barrier of acceptance exists between Turks and Kurds (even though they both speak Turkish in the city) that is great enough to require two distinct church-planting efforts.

Research objectives

• Look for points of contact and acceptance that *do* exist among Turks and Kurds. Are there any? If so, how significant are they?

• Do Turks and Kurds intermarry?

• Describe settlement patterns of Kurdish migrants in the city. Do they live in separate communities? If so, why?

Observation

Living in an urban setting among unreached people groups puts you in an observing posture. You may not know the language, or know it well enough to interact freely with everyone, but you can always observe cultural scenes. Some of your observations may be made just by watching. But the richest observations come while actively participating in life with people. More ideas about participant observation will be described in detail later (see page 52 ff.). A helpful resource would be James P. Spradley's text, *Participant Observation*.

Asking Questions

The time you spend with cultural helpers can be maximized by asking questions related to a particular research topic. By listening well and asking questions, you can learn new things about anything you choose. You can build on what you learn from one cultural helper to the next.

If you interview casually, your friends may not even know that they are being interviewed. Neither will they feel "interrogated" by a nosy foreigner. Specific guidelines for asking questions will also be given soon (see page 65 ff.). For further instruction on interviewing, see James P. Spradley's book *The Ethnographic Interview* and David M. Fetterman's book, *Ethnography Step by Step*.

Understanding

The "U" in the FOQUS cycle reminds us that cultural learning requires time to seriously think about cultural discoveries. Before you know it, you will be swimming in a sea of ideas about the people, their needs, and your dreams for sharing the gospel with them. Our system of writing notes and reading them on a regular basis works to bring understanding to the facts you gather.

Having made observations, asked questions, and recorded your findings, you must move forward by taking the time you need to understand the information you have gathered. Take time to look at your collection of research notes. You will discover what you know and what you don't. Go back and double check what you think you know. Validate the hunches you have by checking them with your cultural helpers. Finally, share your ideas with other workers – with your teammates or others who have lived in your city and ministered there. By comparing your findings and corroborating with others, your base of knowledge becomes even broader and better validated.

Strategizing

Coming up with ministry plans, understanding issues that new converts will face, and actually applying the results of your research in the manner you need is quite exciting. By praying, observing, and asking questions – following the FOQUS cycle – your approach to church planting can be better founded than ever before.

The FOQUS cycle forms a framework for the work and thinking of research. The specific ethnographic skills you will need to go to work fit into this framework. These skills include basic language learning, participant observation, meeting and relating to cultural helpers, ethnographic interviewing, making records of research findings, analyzing and interpreting information, and writing an ethnographic report.

Basic Language Learning

You may be thoroughly enculturated and fluent in the language of the people you desire to study. But if you are not and must carry out the majority of your research in your native language – for example, using English with English-speaking Chinese, Indians, and Malays in Malaysia – you can still use basic language learning skills to aid your research. We have found that basic language learning offers us unique opportunities to connect with people. Even if you only know a few local phrases and speak them incorrectly – with a smile and a pure heart – these phrases will serve as a preface to friendships. Expressing a need to communicate gives people an opportunity to help you. When they realize that they can help you with language, they will often assist you in other ways, such as understanding their culture. A few local phrases spoken correctly can get you places you might not otherwise find. Using them can also make you less conspicuous as you move about the city.

Formal Language Learning

Language acquisition can be done formally and informally. Sometimes we have taken survival language courses during our first several weeks overseas. While some courses have been successful, others have been less helpful. Results vary from individual to individual. Depending on your research situation, formal language courses may help you. Apart from language learning, formal course work provides an often overlooked benefit. A regular schedule and familiar classroom can serve as an anchor in the choppy sea of ambiguity which threatens to overwhelm newcomers to a foreign city.

Informal Language Learning

We have given a great deal more time to *informal* language learning. While other language learning methods are available, we have used a method known by its acronym LAMP. We highly recommend *Language Acquisition Made Practical* by Dr. Thomas Brewster and his wife Elizabeth, as a valuable resource for immersing yourself in a new culture.

It is helpful to learn a native language explanation of your identity and a way to communicate that you are looking for English speakers.

Greatly simplified, the LAMP method can be summed up with an acronym the Brewsters developed: G.L.U.E. It stands for:

G   Get a little.
L   Learn what you get.
U   Use it a lot.
E   Evaluate.

Begin with just a few words and phrases so that you can quickly master them. Don't try to learn too much at once because you will learn little or nothing at all. Learn how to pronounce phrases accurately. You can practice pronunciation by tape-recording short phrases spoken by native speakers. Take the recording home to practice, and don't move on to other phrases until you are fluent in the beginning ones. Use your phrases at every opportunity. As you use them, you

---

Table 4 Language Learning Tips

- *Learn the most appropriate language for your research. For example, if Tajiks are the focus of your study, then Tajik would be the language to learn, even though Russian might be spoken more widely. If you gain even limited proficiency in a minority language, you will more than likely be rewarded by its native speakers. Be cautious if needed – some governments frown on foreigners speaking minority languages.*

- *Learn from those who are fluent in your target language. Preferably, mimic those who speak your target language as their mother tongue.*

- *Learn local phrases rather than translations of English phrases. For example, don't ask how to respond "Oh, not anywhere in particular" when asked, "Where are you going?" A Malay person would not respond that way. They would say, "jalan (jah-**lahn**), jalan," which literally means "road, road."*

- *Learn the language of the street, rather than the formal way of speaking. Native speakers often want to give textbook phrases that only vaguely resemble the way they speak to friends. Learn to speak the way the people speak.*

will create opportunities to expand your contacts. You will find more and more people who are willing to help you learn about their culture. Along the way, evaluate your language ability and the phrases you know or need to know. Continue to add to your language repertoire over time.

Finally, in addition to standard greetings and pleasantries, it is helpful to learn a native language explanation of your identity and a way to communicate that you are looking for English speakers. (e.g., "I am a student from America. I am here to learn about your culture. I am looking for someone who knows a little English to help me.")

Participant Observation

Some say when it comes to negotiating traffic in a foreign land that there are two types of people, the quick and the dead. Newcomers in a city must keep their eyes open and their minds attentive as they go about their business. Likewise, as an ethnographic researcher you must begin your quest with a similar approach: Be watchful while being involved. Navigating in foreign traffic without careful observation could get you killed. But if you simply observe without participating, you will never get to the other side of the street. In ethnography, this skill of *watching* while *doing* is called participant observation. On every occasion, use the following participant observation skills. What you learn by observing can be fed back into the FOQUS cycle – generating new research goals and better questions to ask.

The skill of watching while doing is called participant observation.

Life everywhere consists of participation in various activities: going to work, buying food, and interacting with friends and family. Everyone participates – even in new settings overseas. A participant observer, however, is unique in three significant ways.

Dual Purpose

Participant observers carry out a dual purpose. Not only do they participate in an activity, they also watch to learn all they can about what transpires. Let's say that you are invited to a wedding during your third week in the country. You consider this an honor and gladly attend. While you enjoy the festivities and friendship, you also keep your eyes open to learn all that such an event can tell you about the culture you are studying.

Eyes Wide Open

Participant observers watch thoroughly and broadly. When too much information bombards you, you screen most of it out. The potential for sensory overload is *increased* when you are in a foreign culture. But to be an effective participant observer you must endeavor to see everything that is happening. In his book, *Participant Observation*, James P. Spradley writes, "Increasing your awareness does not come easily, for you must overcome years of selective inattention, tuning out, not seeing, and not hearing."

A good participant observer looks at a situation with a wide angle lens. Rather than focusing on a certain person or interesting activity, you must take in the whole environment.

For example, when you are hurrying to catch a commuter train to the other side of the city, you might only see the timetable and the platform number, indicating when and where to find your train. But if you take a moment to look around, you might see beggars soliciting on the stairway, wealthy businessmen sidestepping them or donating to them, porters wearing distinct uniforms vying to carry belongings for families just arriving from the countryside, and hawkers selling food to the police who are overseeing the whole scene. Much can be learned and many questions raised simply by widening the scope of information you allow yourself to receive.

Preserve What You See

Participant observers *record* their observations. Rather than simply passing through the events of life, try to preserve what you see, what you feel about what you see, and the questions it raises for you. The upcoming section on notetaking will equip you to do this (see page 71 ff.).

Participant observation provides an important tool for you to begin understanding the culture you are studying. Through involved watchfulness, you can begin to discern the issues that merit further investigation. Later on in your course of study, participant observation may confirm or disprove your ideas about particular missiological problems.

Sharing in the daily lives and activities of the people you want to understand also leads you to significant information you might not otherwise uncover. Involvement tends to help you develop an insider status, allowing access to insights denied to outsiders. In his book, *Participant Observation: A Methodology for Human Studies*, Danny L. Jorgensen writes,

> *Most human settings ... do not give up the insider's world of meaning and action except to a person willing to become a member. The deeper meanings of most forms of human existence are not displayed for outsiders. They are available primarily to people for whom these meanings constitute a way of life* (page 60).

Putting Participant Observation Skills to Work

In Turkish culture, boys are circumcised between the ages of five and ten. The event is called a sunet.

To understand how to implement participant observation in your study of an unreached people, let's consider a social situation and how you might learn from it. In Turkish culture, boys take a significant step into manhood when they are circumcised between the ages of five and ten. The event is called a *sunet*. For a typical *sunet*, friends and family parade the boy through the streets of the city with rousing drums and trumpets. A festive party, with as many as one hundred guests, is thrown after the actual circumcision. Tables full of food nourish the revelers as they dance late into the night. The five or six hours that the *sunet* lasts would be a great time to use participant observation skills. The quantity and quality of information you might gain would be affected by three variables.

Level of Participation

Your participant observation could range from non-participation to active participation. Let's briefly examine each.

Non-involvement

At this level you might observe an aspect of culture second-hand. You might watch a Turkish language documentary about *sunets*. Though you might not understand the commentator, you would see the activity associated with a *sunet*.

Passive Participation

At this level you would simply stand by and watch. Let's say you stumble upon a *sunet* caravan noisily parading down the street. If you watch the activity, perhaps follow the caravan for awhile, but don't participate in the celebration – your participation would be passive. This level can easily lead to a higher level. If someone in the *sunet* caravan invites you to ride along with them, you would be elevated to the next level.

Moderate Participation

At this level, a participant observer is somewhere between being an insider and an outsider. If you have only been in the culture for a short time, this may be the best level for you because you can absorb a good deal of the new information assaulting you.

Active Participation

At this level you would do what the people are doing. If you were actually at the *sunet* you would learn to do the dances, eat and laugh with friends, and congratulate (or perhaps console) the newly circumcised boy. During this time it may be appropriate for you to ask some simple questions regarding what you see.

Scope of Observation

The type and amount of information you can gain from participant observation is also governed by what you decide to observe. When you begin your research, take the broadest view possible. Drink in all the new sights and sounds that bombard you. For example, at a *sunet* observe the number of people attending, their apparent age and relationship, the sequence of events, the food served to the guests, and the setting chosen for the celebration.

Later, you might focus your observation on a particular aspect of a social event. Narrow your scope of observation so that you can concentrate and move deeper in your understanding. Be careful not to focus too early as this might cause you to overlook important areas of study. Using the *sunet* example, you might focus your observation on the people present. Watch to answer such questions as: Who arrives when? What do they wear? How are various guests treated by the host? How are different people involved in the ceremony of circumcision?

The most limited scope of observation is called selective observation. If you take a selective view of the *sunet*, you might watch to understand the differences in activity and involvement between men and women. Observe their various roles and the way others respond to them. Your observations could shed significant insights on the roles and interactions of families in Turkish culture.

Strategic Approach

A third variable affecting participant observation is strategic approach. Your physical and social location, as well as your ability to work as a team, are components of taking a strategic approach.

Physical Location

To be a good participant observer, go where the action is. Find good observation posts from which to view activities of the city. Follow crowds and visit gathering points. If you might learn new things, humbly ask to be admitted to an event. For instance, before joining a *sunet* you may have simply been on your way to the post office when you saw a commotion down a side street. You must choose between going on your way or investigating. Upon arriving at the celebration, you may have to approach someone and ask, "Excuse me, can you tell me what's going on here? Can I come in?" Pursue a variety of vantage points in the city. Important new vistas will be opened for you.

Social Location

Your ability to gain access to a social situation and to understand it is greatly affected by who introduces you to the situation. Your status in a new setting will reflect that of your sponsor. For instance, your insider status at the *sunet* would be less if you accompanied a guest than if you had been invited by the circumcised boy's father.

Team work

A variety of people participating in the same event will come away with a variety of observations. For example, if you are a woman you mieter opportunity to observe the mother's role at the *sunet*. A man on the other hand, might observe the circumcision more closely – and wince with empathy. If you are doing research as a team, take advantage of everyone's observations.

Participant observation is an important activity throughout the research cycle. Properly employed, it will bring relevant questions to the surface and shed light on the perplexing issues you face.

To be a participant observer, go where the action is.

Selecting and Relating to Cultural Helpers

Cultural helpers are people who help you see their culture through their eyes.

Our experience of carrying out research in more than thirty settings has been a rich, collective experience. We owe a great debt to the many cultural helpers who have joined us in our work to understand their cities, their peoples, and their way of life. Cultural helpers are people who help you see their culture through their eyes. Without them, even the best research methods would remain lifeless.

Finding cultural helpers is a necessary prerequisite to asking questions. And asking questions is the means we use to unravel the mystery of "Who are the peoples?" "What are they like?" and "How can they be reached?" Selecting good cultural helpers is a matter of knowing *what* to look for and *where* to look for it. A good cultural helper will exhibit certain character

What To Look For

Thorough enculturation

Good cultural helpers should be insiders in the community they are telling you about. They should be thoroughly familiar with the culture you are studying. Thorough enculturation increases your ability to gain an emic (insider's) perspective.

Current involvement

An emic perspective also depends on cultural helpers who are presently insiders in the community. Things change. A cultural helper who has been absent for a number of years may no longer be up to date. Those, however, who are currently involved can give more accurate information.

Available

The most insightful cultural helpers will be of little help if they lack the time to spend talking with you. Good cultural helpers should have sufficient time and be willing to share it with you.

Non-analytical

Good cultural helpers shouldn't analyze your questions and present information to you in academic terms. They should tell you what they see and believe without anticipating your conclusions.

Finding people who meet these qualifications requires a combination of divine intervention, common sense, and perseverance. We encourage you to pray – beginning in the earliest stages of your research project – that God will arrange friends for you in your target city. Dependence on God is needed even in the practical aspects of using research skills. The following five steps will help you find quality cultural helpers.

Universities, schools, and bookstores may be good sources for quality cultural helpers.

"Troll" the Streets

Walk through areas you want to research to approach people and initiate conversations. You may have to repeat your efforts to successfully locate a cultural helper. We call this method "trolling" after the fishing method of the same name. While it may seem haphazard, this method exposes you to new people, and it has, in fact, netted some extraordinary cultural helpers for us.

Go Where the Getting Is Good

Go where English speakers are likely to be found. Universities, schools, and bookstores may be good sources for quality cultural helpers. Some professions may also have a high number of English speakers. Of course, tourist sites are usually staffed by people who speak English. These folks can be quite helpful. Some, though, are only interested in selling you their goods and services.

Formal Arrangements

In some situations, university personnel or tourist officials may be able to arrange contacts with English speakers. These officials can be particularly helpful in a city with very few potential helpers.

Your Friend's Friends

Make an effort to meet the people your cultural helper spends time with. These can be family, other relatives, schoolmates, co-workers, or friends. Not only will this expand your pool of cultural helpers, it will give you valuable insight into your friend.

Use a Translator

Sometimes translation is necessary to find cultural helpers from certain groups of people. For example, the only way to speak to an elderly man or a marginalized group of nomads may be with a translator. In this situation, take care to speak to your new cultural helper, rather than to the translator. Ask the translator to tell you word for word what the new cultural helper says. Researchers sometimes ask a question through translation and wait expectantly through a passionate, five minute reply, only to have the translator turn and report, "he says, 'No.'"

The key to finding good cultural helpers is talking to numerous people. Keep in mind that you may have to kiss a lot of frogs before you find a prince. This aspect of the research can be trying. Nearly everyone feels uncomfortable approaching a stranger to start a conversation. Even veteran Caleb Project researchers take time to get used to initiating conversations with strangers. But that is how we meet good cultural helpers.

Relationships of Trust

Cultural helpers rarely provide significant information outside the context of a trusting relationship. Think of your relationship with a cultural helper as a bridge and the information he or she gives you as a load being carried across that bridge. The heavier, or more significant, you want the information to be, the stronger the bridge must be. You can build trust with your cultural helper by explaining what you want to learn and how you think he or she can help you. Spending time with a cultural helper and sharing about yourself and your life also builds trust.

Sometimes in the course of a research project, it becomes necessary to move on from one cultural helper to another. This sometimes occurs when the focus of research shifts to a group in which your cultural helper is not an insider. While it is important to be kind and sensitive to your friends, it is unwise to solicit information from people who cannot give it. To face this situation in a wise and godly manner, consider the following three guidelines:

- *Value your friend enough to explain what is happening. Don't just stop seeing him or her.*

- *Respect your cultural helpers throughout your relationship. At parting, neither of you should feel as though your cultural helper has been used. Since you benefit from their information, they should benefit from your friendship. Take time to answer their questions and to help them improve their English. In some cases, it may be appropriate to pay cultural helpers, particularly if you ask them to translate on a regular basis.*

- *Even though someone is no longer a cultural helper, he or she can remain a friend. Caleb Project researchers sometimes spend their free days with former cultural helpers – not to gain more information, but to continue a friendship.*

How To Avoid Wasting Time

Improper selection of cultural helpers can result in wasted time or even in danger to you. Our experience over several years has highlighted three main pitfalls you may face in choosing cultural helpers.

Insufficient English

English speaking cultural helpers are essential unless researchers use a local language fluently. A person may fit all the characteristics of a good cultural helper, but if he or she is unable to communicate with you, you should move on. In some cases you may choose to sit back and observe or use a translator.

Too many hours can be lost trying to communicate in sign language or with limited English. Again, this pitfall says nothing about the character of potential cultural helpers. They may be wonderful friends, but contribute little to the research. One Caleb Project researcher spent many hours on her free days in a home where no English was spoken. No interview information was gathered but her relationship with the family fueled her vision and burden for the church to grow in Turkey.

"Fringe" People

Be watchful for cultural helpers who live on the fringe of society. You want to understand the main flow of a culture, the broad beliefs and values by which most people live. People who don't live their lives by those beliefs and values cannot share an insider's perspective with you. Look instead for cultural helpers who are representative of the population. The most worthwhile and reliable insights often come from the most average people.

Watch Out For the Safety of Others, And For Yourself

Sometimes simply speaking to an American can cause your cultural helper to be questioned by the authorities. Take precautions not to endanger your friends and helpers.

As a researcher you may come under suspicion for your activities. Sometimes we have been presumed guilty of crimes simply by association. Once, two researchers were taken to the police station because they unknowingly stumbled into a drug dealer's territory. Also watch for, and avoid, cultural helpers with strong anti-government sentiments or other subversive, fundamental, or extremist ideas.

Putting these guidelines into effect help you obtain a number of excellent cultural helpers. Now that you have them, what do you do with them?

Interviewing

Ethnographic interviews are the fundamental unit of Caleb Project Research. Interviewing adds to participant observation and provides the vast majority of information we unearth. An ethnographic interview done well feels much like an ordinary conversation, but in the process, it answers many of your questions. In fact, the person you have the most fun with may be the best person to interview.

So much information is available, locked up in the minds and hearts of each person in every city. It is there, if you will but ask. Your questions not only get information for you, they also honor those whom you ask. You invite cultural helpers to share themselves, their beliefs, opinions, values, loves, and hates. When you listen, you validate their experiences and thoughts.

Step One: Initiate a Conversation

To conduct an ethnographic interview, you must have someone to talk to. As research progresses, more and more of your interviews will be with people to whom you have already spoken. You will return to specific people because of what you already know about them. Their ethnic background, their occupation, or perhaps their religious affiliation will coincide with your present topic. Or you will seek them out to follow up on a previous conversation or to confirm information you have learned from others.

At the outset of your research project, however, new relationships must be initiated. For some researchers this poses the greatest challenge to understanding a city or a people. The previous section discussed where to find good cultural helpers and what to look for. But having located good cultural helpers, you must

At the outset of your research project, new relationships must be initiated.

know how to approach them. We have used the following ways to sensitively initiate conversations with cultural helpers.

Try to Learn the Language

Most people reward foreigners' efforts to learn their language. Approach someone and ask whether they can tell you how to say something. This often opens the door to a conversation and may eventually lead to a relationship. A classic example of this approach is asking a fellow bus rider how to tell the driver to stop. In the early days in a new city, also ask how to say appropriate greetings and courtesy phrases.

Note that initiating a conversation with, "Do you speak English?" is rarely successful. The response to this question will almost always be negative, even though the person may speak quite passable English. If you simply ask a question in English, the response will demonstrate the presence or absence of English ability.

Have a Need

The easiest way to initiate a conversation with a potential cultural helper is to express a need. People in most places are willing to help a foreigner who is obviously in need. Needs do not have to be complicated. You can ask how to order food, how to find the right bus, or how much a pay phone costs.

You can initiate a conversation based specifically on the needs you have as a newcomer to a city. You might approach someone and say, "Excuse me, I'm new here. Could you help me find the post office?" Or, "I've just arrived in your city and need to rent a room. Could you help me find housing?"

Use A Direct Approach

Sometimes preliminaries must be thrown aside and a direct approach is appropriate. For example, to a new cultural helper you might say, "Excuse me. Could you help me? I'm from America and I would like to learn about your city."

Use Your Current Situation

Conversations can often be initiated by simply asking the person next to you about something you see. Point to a building, a statue, or a crowd of people and ask, "Excuse me, what is that? What is happening over there?"

Step Two: Build Rapport

Once you have initiated a conversation with a potential cultural helper, you should begin to build rapport. An ethnographic interview is much more like a friendly conversation than a news interview. You will not gain deep insights into a culture by interrogating your cultural helpers. They may know that you are pursuing specific understanding of their culture, but the questions you ask should feel like they are coming from an interested friend, not a reporter.

Several strategies can be employed to build rapport. Keep in mind that your cultural helper will sense your attitude. If you merely use your cultural helper to reach your goals, you lack kindness. Your insights will most likely be shallow. If cultural helpers perceive that you *do* care about them and want to get to know them, the friendship will deepen.

Move Slow And Stay Low

Because most cultures operate on more subtle levels, it is important for foreigners (especially Americans) to tone down their approach when first getting to know a cultural helper. The accepted hearty, "Hello" and firm handshake may communicate the right message to fellow Americans, but in some cultures it causes potentially fine cultural helpers to turn and flee down the sidewalk. A slow and low approach will be much more effective. For example, we found in Thailand that we needed to physically bend down a bit before softly asking, "Excuse me, could you help me?"

A second aspect of the slow and low strategy concerns the questions that are asked during the first few minutes of an interview. Aim for questions that are

Laughing together is a sure sign of rapport.

culturally acceptable, non-threatening, and easy to answer. People generally enjoy answering questions about their family and occupation. Wait until later to broach subjects such as religious practice and ethnic tension. You can ease into sensitive themes by first asking what most people think or do regarding a subject. Later, ask your cultural helper what he or she personally thinks or does.

Play The Name Game

A second key to building rapport is choosing the right time to exchange names. Introductions that occur too early can be intimidating, while waiting too long communicates that the conversation is an anonymous affair that will not be repeated. Look for opportunities to ask your cultural helper's name. At some point you might say, "Here I am talking to you, my friend, and I don't even know your name. I am John." Follow up an introduction with the local language version of "I'm so glad to make your acquaintance." If the conversation comes to a close and you have not exchanged names, but want to, face the clumsiness and ask outright. People will often be pleased by your interest if you ask them for their name and phone number so you can be sure to see them again.

Use Laugh Lines

Laughing together is a sure sign of rapport. One Caleb Project researcher commented, "If I can get them to laugh, I know I have a friend." As with exchanging names, laughing too early in a conversation can seem artificial and presumptuous, but at the right time it can communicate, "We are friends and we sure enjoy each other's company." A researcher's main source of humor will likely be himself. Don't be afraid to laugh at your clumsiness with the local language and culture. Encourage your cultural helper to join in.

Step Three: Asking Questions

As mentioned above, an ethnographic interview should have the character of a friendly conversation. At the same time, you should have goals in mind, areas you want to pursue and specific understanding you want to gain. These goals and areas of interest are presented in detail in Part III. But before we introduce these, let's explore the basics of ethnographic interviewing. Skillful interviewing takes practice and discernment. The following guidelines will help.

Push and Relax

Like a normal conversation with a good friend, an ethnographic interview will vary in intensity. It should flow seamlessly between times of fervent discussion and periods of light dialogue and back again through variations of the two. At times you push the conversation to ask progressively deeper or more personal questions. But watch for clues that it is time to back off and enjoy less intense chatting. One Caleb Project researcher struggled to find a good balance between the two. Her cultural helper playfully told her that she was too serious, that she should have more fun.

Ride and Guide

Unlike a regular conversation, which proceeds at the whim of the two participants, you are the primary conductor in an ethnographic interview. You set the direction for the conversation. In the normal pattern of an interview, you have a general direction in mind, toward which you subtly but persistently guide the conversation. Sometimes, however, a conversation will get happily out of hand. Your cultural helper will race off toward areas of his or her own choosing. As a wise researcher, discern whether these directions are beneficial or not. An exhaustive history of Islam may not contribute to the research problem at hand, but a lengthy discourse on the origin of your cultural helper's community, while unasked for, might unlock rich insights. When this is true, go from guiding the conversation to riding it. Riding a conversation is like sledding on ice. You know you are connected to the objectives of your interview, but at least for a while, you are out of control, following an unpredictable course. In time, you will again move to a position of guiding the conversation.

An ethnographic interview should have the character of a friendly conversation.

Pursue Themes

Start an interview with general areas of inquiry, rather than beginning with a list of specific questions. This mental distinction will help you go from point to point in response to your cultural helper's answers. Don't arbitrarily go down your list of research questions. Ask follow-up questions; they will help you pursue a theme. When cultural helpers answer questions, ask them for clarification, for what else they know about the subject, or about related areas. Go on to the next question only when the previous one has been exhausted.

Leave Gracefully

The time will come when an ethnographic interview draws to a close. Either you or your cultural helper must leave, or you both have run out of things to talk about. At this point, take care that three things happen. First, leave graciously and in a culturally appropriate manner. Second, express gratitude to your cultural helper. Tell him how helpful he was, and thank him for sharing his time and insight. Third, make arrangements for a subsequent meeting, or at least make sure the door is open for further contact. This may involve setting a time and place, or it may mean getting a phone number or address. However you work it out, do not leave a good cultural helper without a way to contact him again.

Types of Questions

Three general types of questions comprise an ethnographic interviewer's repertoire. They are descriptive questions, structural questions, and contrast questions. In the course of an interview, all three types can be used in any combination. However, on a given topic of inquiry, descriptive questions have a broad focus while structural and contrast questions have a narrower focus.

Descriptive Questions

Descriptive questions consist of general requests for information. Use them to explore the general contours of a topic of interest in fairly comprehensive detail. These questions give you a broad picture of a cultural helper's world.

Descriptive questions are usually used at the beginning of an interview or to initiate new topics of inquiry. They provide a good starting place to look for a cultural helper's own ideas. They also make the cultural helper feel comfortable and knowledgeable.

When using descriptive questions, ask your cultural helper to talk about things which interest you. For instance, "Tell me about this neighborhood," or, "Tell me about the festival that is taking place this week." Four types of descriptive questions should be noted.

Grand Tour Questions

These descriptive questions ask for a broad overview of some matter of interest. Essentially, they ask the cultural helper to give the researcher a grand tour of a particular topic. For instance, you might open the topic of religion with the following grand tour question, "Tell me about people's religious beliefs or feelings about the supernatural."

Mini Tour Questions

These involve a more detailed exploration of a particular matter. For example you would ask a Muslim, "You mentioned that many Muslims live in this city. What do they believe about the supernatural or miracles?"

Experience Questions

These ask for illustrations from people's first hand experience. For example, "You said that Muslims believe in evil spirits. Have you or any of your friends ever had an encounter with an evil spirit? Could you describe what happened?"

RLB

I asked Jamal to tell me about <*goothdigme*> (the evil eye). She explained that it has happened to her two times. Jamal was invited to a friend's house. She went and didn't know some of the people. She took an instant dislike to one woman on the basis of her looks. When Jamal was eating, she started feeling very ill. She left early and was sick for a few days. She said xxx I don't like to go to parties because I may not know all the people there. Perhaps I will get <*goothdigme*>. And you know, when a person is ill the doctor will give his diagnosis of a cold or a stomach problem. This is silly. When it's <*goothdigme*> the doctor cannot treat it. What's the use? He cannot help. yyy

Filenote Excerpt: Example of a descriptive question.

Native Language Questions

These descriptive questions request explanations of particular local terms, concepts, or phrases. For instance, "You mentioned that when someone has an evil spirit in them, you take them to the *Bomah*. Tell me about the *Bomah*. What is it?"

Using Descriptive Questions

Descriptive questions are fairly easy to use in an ethnographic interview. But we have found even greater success in using them when we lengthen the question.

This often results in longer answers. Instead of asking, "Can you tell me about religion here?" ask, "Can you help me understand religion in your city? What is it like? I know very little about the beliefs of people who live here or how they practice them. Can you tell me?" Although using more words may sound strange, it communicates to cultural helpers that you are truly interested in their ideas.

Describing the Berbers of Casablanca

The numerous Berber tribes of Morocco can be divided into three main groups. These are the Rif, the Middle Atlas, and the Southern Berbers. Each of these groups have their own language and culture.

The Rif Berbers come from the mountains in the north of the country and are known for their toughness and hardness, their tradition as successful warriors, and for being men of their word. In their homeland they are resistant to outside influence, even to the Moroccan government, and in many ways practice a law unto themselves. There are very few Rif Berbers in the capital city of Casablanca because most Rif who leave their homeland do so to work in Europe.

The Middle Atlas Berbers come from the mountains in the middle of the country. Although there are Middle Atlas Berbers in Casablanca, they are the least distinct of the Berber groups and tend to mix with the general population. There are, however, a large number of them in the army.

Southern Berbers are generally honest, hard working, and devout Muslims. They are known for their good character. They tend to trust one another more than outsiders. Family ties are important, and even after moving to Casablanca, Southern Berbers make frequent trips home.

When using descriptive questions, be careful not to ask leading questions. Such questions lead your cultural helper to respond to categories of your own making rather than letting her suggest her own. For example, it is better to ask "Who lives here?" than to ask, "What kinds of people live here?" The second question is a leading question because it assumes that there are different kinds of people. The cultural helper will be predisposed to think of kinds of people, rather than use her own way to talk about people in her neighborhood.

Avoid leading questions because they can skew your understanding of the culture. Also, try to avoid questions that will result in "yes" or "no" answers. These are usually unproductive.

Also beware of asking overwhelming questions like, "Can you tell me all of the languages spoken here?" Instead ask, "What are some of the languages spoken here?" After the cultural helper responds, ask, "Do you know of any others?" This fully taps your cultural helper's knowledge without embarrassing or intimidating him.

Structural Questions

Structural questions follow on the heels of descriptive questions. They are used to discover more about what you have learned in response to descriptive questions. For example, if you ask your cultural helper to tell you about her neighborhood (a descriptive question), you should follow her response with a structural question. A structural question might be, "You mentioned that there are Cutchi Memons and Halai Memons, *are there any other types of Memons?*" If you are talking in general about Memon families, a related structural question would be, "What are some of the family problems that are common in the Memon community?" As your cultural helper answers descriptive questions, you should consider what structural questions you want to ask next.

Use structural questions carefully. They are rarely used in a friendly conversation and tend to make an interview feel more formal. This effect can be countered to some degree by asking structural questions in the midst of broader descriptive questions.

Contrast Questions

Contrast questions are used to discover and clarify meaning. They help you understand the relationships and differences between terms a cultural helper has described. For instance, "What are the differences between people who speak Russian and Uzbek?" and, "You mentioned Rif Berbers, Middle Atlas Berbers, and Southern Berbers. How do they compare to one another?"

Other Lines of Questioning

In addition to the three basic types of ethnographic questions, other lines of questioning can be valuable.

Folk Tales

People often use folk tales to transmit cultural values and lessons from one generation to the next. Folk tales provide insight into the secular and the sacred, the intellectual and the emotional life of a people. Jokes also illustrate deeply held feelings and convictions. We generally stumble onto folk tales and jokes by accident. You may, however, ask specifically about these things.

A Kazakh Folk Tale

There once was a very wise man. He was respected by all the people in the village. When he was about to die he called his son in and gave him three bits of advice: never greet the elders in the village, eat only the most delicious foods, and love only the prettiest women. The father then died and the son set out to follow his father's advice. He would ride past the elders in the village and not say anything. He killed all of the best animals and ate them for food. He also loved only the prettiest women in the village.

The people in the village began to ask why the son of such a wise man would behave in such a foolish way. What was the meaning of the father's advice?

The father meant for the son to go to work early in the morning and return late at night so he would not be able to greet the elders in the village. After such a hard day's work, any food would taste delicious, therefore he would only be eating delicious food. And finally, if he were to work hard, he'd see few people during the day so that his wife and sisters would be the most lovely women he saw. Therefore he would only love the prettiest women.

Life histories

Cultural helpers can provide rich, detailed autobiographical descriptions. These life histories are usually quite personal. How a cultural helper weaves a personal story, however, tells much about the fabric of a social group. To initiate a life history, ask, "Could you tell me the story of how you and your family came to live here?" or, "Things must have changed a great deal since you were young. Can you tell me about the changes?"

Interviewing Tips

The following tips will help you ask ethnographic questions effectively.

- *Repeat explanations about what you want to learn. "As I mentioned earlier, I want to learn about Arab families. I was wondering, can you tell me the role of a father in an Arab family?"*

- *Repeat questions or ask variations of the same questions. This will draw responses that shed new light on the topic. Scatter repeated questions throughout the interview, rather than asking them back to back.*

- *Speak slowly and clearly. Wait for a response before restating your question. Encourage cultural helpers to speak without making them feel uncomfortable or threatened.*

- *Use silence skillfully. Avoid filling in by offering multiple choices. Though none of your choices may be correct, one of them will likely be chosen.*

- *Occasionally ask cultural helpers to repeat descriptions. This will communicate that you are especially interested and want to understand them better. This also helps you get a second look at matters of interest and to correct misunderstandings.*

- *Similarly, it is useful to restate what your cultural helper said to ensure that you heard correctly.*

- *Limit "why" questions. Sometimes they sound judgmental, as though you are questioning your cultural helper's motives. If necessary, ask for use, rather than meaning. Instead of, "Why would you do that?" ask, "When would you do that?"*

- *Watch for impression management. Cultural helpers will often shade the truth to tell you what they think you want to hear. Or, they may tell you what they want you to believe, regardless of the truth. If you suspect that impression management is occurring, make note of it in your records.*

- *Recognize your own cultural biases. Don't presume that you understand what you are researching. Delay making judgments so that you can incorporate more information.*

Making Records of Research Findings

Imagine that it is your first week in Tashkent, Uzbekistan, and you are invited to your Uzbek neighbor's apartment for tea. You have passed various members of the family in the stairwell a number of times, but you are struggling to put names to faces. You are quite sure that the family is curious about what you are doing – they seem open and helpful. When you enter their front room, you are invited to sit on a carpet with everyone. A veritable feast lies before your eyes – not just tea, but a national dish called *pilau* is piled on a huge tray, surrounded by watermelon, nuts, and stacks of Uzbek bread called *nan*. After three hours of talking back and forth, you participate in a ceremony that is particularly interesting. The eldest man in the room – your neighbor's uncle who lives on a collective farm outside the city – bows his head and raises his arms to chant a prayer, or *oman,* in Arabic. After the chant has drifted to silence and everyone has brought their hands down over their faces, you realize the meal is finished.

Later, back at home, the richness of all you learned in three short hours seems to escape to the hidden recesses of your mind. What did the father say about his job? And what was that about the uncle's wife being out of town to visit – what

What could you have done to remember and record your experience with this warm Uzbek family?

his name? Was he a healer or magician of some kind? Now more questions than solid facts fill your mind and the details are lost. What could you have done to remember and record your first experience with this warm Uzbek family?

To record your experiences you will need to write notes. According to James P. Spradley, there are four kinds of fieldnotes: condensed, expanded, journal, and analysis and interpretation notes. All four kinds are helpful and easy to write – especially if you develop and use an adequate system. If you are working with a team, each member can use the same notetaking system and efficiently pool their information. The system we have developed includes all four types of notes and it is easy to use. While lap top computers and printers can be extremely helpful for making records, these tools are not absolutely necessary. You can write notes by hand.

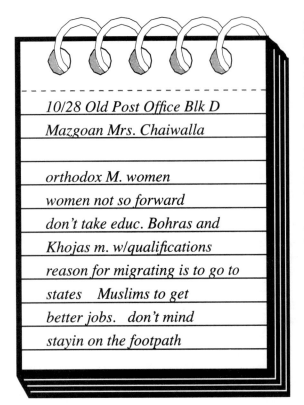

10/28 Old Post Office Blk D

Mazgoan Mrs. Chaiwalla

orthodox M. women

women not so forward

don't take educ. Bohras and

Khojas m. w/qualifications

reason for migrating is to go to

states   Muslims to get

better jobs.   don't mind

stayin on the footpath

Sample Fieldnote

Condensed Notes

Writing condensed notes (we call it "taking fieldnotes") is done on location when you are with cultural helpers. The purpose of these notes is to jot down reminders of conversations and observation situations.

For a field notebook, we use a pocket-sized spiral notepad. They are convenient to carry in your pants pocket or purse – we take them everywhere we go, in addition to a pencil. Every time you go out, *carry a small notebook with you.*

The biggest obstacle to notetaking is taking out your notepad and explaining it to your cultural helper. We often say something like, "I am trying to be a good learner. But I am learning so much, and I am so forgetful, I need to write things down. Do you mind if I write in my notebook while we talk together?" If taking notes during a conversation is inappropriate, jot notes immediately afterward. Sometimes frequent bathroom trips help you take notes out of sight.

Tips for Using a Field Notebook

• *Avoid pulling out your notebook abruptly or without an adequate explanation. This will cause your cultural helper unnecessary stress. Until you explain, your helper won't have any idea why you are writing things down. If possible, bring your notebook out with an explanation at the beginning of an interview. This way, your helper quickly forgets the notebook while it remains available for your use*

Other natural times to pull out your notebook might be to record a new language term, to spell a word, or to jot down a name, address, or phone number.

- *Always write the name of your cultural helper and the date at the beginning of the note. Their address and phone number should also be recorded if it is your first meeting, as this will be particularly helpful if you want to contact the person again.*

- *Be careful about who holds your notebook. If you have taken notes to yourself that allude to church planting, you may jeopardize your own security by letting others read it.*

- *Don't lose, throw away, or tear pages out of a notebook. You will want to refer to them later.*

Working as Partners

Taking notes is especially difficult when you are alone with a number of people or with a family. We always interview in pairs as "teamlet partners." One partner asks questions and actively participates in the conversation while the other partner takes notes. If you have the good fortune of working with a partner, decide beforehand who will take notes and who will interview. This avoids confusion. You can always switch roles if one of you tires of talking or listening.

Interviewing partners can also help notetaking partners by repeating parts of the conversation. For example, let's say you ask a question like, "You just mentioned a new word that I haven't heard before – *tebip*. Could you tell me what *tebip* is?" This slows the conversation, and having heard the word three times (once from the cultural helper and twice from the interviewer) the notetaker can more easily write everything down. When a conversation wanes, the interviewer can also ask the notetaker, "Have you thought of additional questions that we could ask?"

Principles of Notetaking

A helpful principle for taking interview notes is the verbatim principle. The verbatim principle is taking notes so that *what people say* is recorded. Even when you don't understand terms people use, write down exactly what they say – verbatim. This helps reduce your tendency to inject ideas that come from personal or cultural biases.

When Should You Take Notes?

Write fieldnotes during each interview that you have and for each participant observation situation you encounter. For example, take notes when you are invited to tea or to a wedding. Take notes when you meet with national believers and other Christian workers. Take notes when collecting library research. Add all types of information to your collection of research notes just as you would add direct interview or observation information. In general, fieldnotes are incomprehensible to everyone but the notetaker. For this reason, fieldnotes are later expanded into "filenotes."

Expanded Notes

By taking fieldnotes you prepare yourself to write expanded notes. We call expanded notes "filenotes." Writing filenotes from fieldnotes is the most accurate way to record what you learn. Filenotes also allow you to share what you have learned with others – particularly in a team situation. If possible, save time by composing and printing filenotes on a lap top computer and printer.

Filenotes are a re-creation of an interview. Using your fieldnotes as a reminder, write down information just as it was shared with you. There are two logical approaches to writing filenotes: the chronological and the topical. You may write a filenote the way the conversation occurred – that is, in order. Or, you may write it one topic at a time. For example, from one interview you might pull together everything about marriage, then everything about neighborhoods, etc.

After interviewing, use your fieldnotes to re-create the interview in filenote format.

A 24-Hour Rule applies to filenote writing. Within twenty-four hours of an interview, expand your fieldnotes into filenotes. If you wait any longer, your ability to re-create the interview will be hindered.

Besides recording an interview, use filenotes for recording your own comments about what you learn. Personal comments should be kept separate from the record of the interview itself. A general format that is easy to follow includes 1) the Heading, 2) the Filenote Body, and 3) Your Comments (see Sample Filenote).

Sample Filenote

EMJP0321B
Name: Farhad (and his friend Bassar)

Context:
        We were trolling in Midan and met Farhad inside his paper supply shop.

^^^^^

NBR
        Farhad lives in the neighborhood called Midan (mee-don). The name means
bravery, which was displayed during the French occupation. There are heroes in each
neighborhood. People take pride in their neighborhoods.
        Everything is centered from Old Damascus. That is the important thing in the
city: how things relate to Old Damascus.

FAM, NBR
        Farhad said his family has been in Damascus for about 300 years which they
can account for. Basam said his family has been here for 500 years, substantiated.
They said it is very good to be from Damascus like that, to be "Shamee."

ASI
        Basam said that there is an organization, a club in Damascus for the
very old families. He thought it is called the Damascus Club. He said it is
very exclusive, and he doesn't know a whole lot about it. He said he has heard
that some families in it go back 700 years or more. He wasn't sure how many
were in the club.

vvvvv

What Happened
        Both Farhad and Basam were proud to tell about their lineage in Damascus. It
was like a "I can beat that, my family has been here for 500 years."

So What
        Neighborhoods seem to be more important to Shamee than to others –
especially their connection to Old Damascus. If there really is a club for Shamee,
it could lead to understanding social gatherings for Shamee, and give ideas about
church planting.

What Next
        Talk to more Shamee and find out how important it is to them to be Shamee,
and to live with or near other Shamee. Find out how exclusive their relationships
are. Ask about the Damascus Club. Is it real? Who is in it, and how many? What is it
like? Perhaps we should visit the club if we can.

The Heading

Filenote headings are helpful reference items. The first line is a Filenote ID which includes the interviewer and notetaker's initials, the date of the interview, and the number of the interview for that day (e.g., "A" for first interview, "B" for second interview, etc.). The second line contains the names of cultural helpers who were a part of the conversation. Additional information after the first two lines can be included, such as where the interview took place or more specific information about the cultural helper. This might be useful if notes will be read by other team members.

The Filenote Body

The main text of the interview can be organized using topic headings. Our list of topic headings correspond to many of the topics discussed in Part III and may be used as a starting point for your own work. However, they are only guides. Develop additional three-letter topic headings to fit your setting and situation.

Topic headings help when you want to read filenotes about a particular topic. For example, when you want to read notes about marriage, you can locate the MAR headings.

When writing filenotes, include your cultural helpers' words. What they say should be recorded with minimal "translation" on your part. Set apart native terms with brackets (e.g., <*goothdigme*>) and quotations with an "XXX" at the beginning and "YYY" at the end of a verbatim statement (see Sample Filenote on page 67). These tags make it easier to compile quotes for analysis and writing.

Table 5 A Selection of Topic Headings

CLS	Class	EDC	Education
ETH	Ethnicity	NTW	Networks
LNG	Language and dialects	KIN	Kinship
NBR	Neighborhood	MAR	Marriage
OCC	Occupation	ASI	Associations & Institutions
RLB	Religious Beliefs	LDR	Leadership
RLP	Religious Practice	URB	Urbanization
FAM	Family	GOV	Government
POL	Politics	ECN	Economy
CST	Caste or tribal groups	CMN	Communication
REO	Region of origin	HST	history
SEC	Secularization	DEM	Demographics/Statistics
MOD	Modernization	EVG	history of Evangelization
MIG	Stage of migration	CHG	Church Growth
		REC	Receptivity

Your Comments

A section of the filenote is set apart for your comments. Whereas the main text strictly contains the facts of an interview, the comment section contains your analysis, interpretation, and questions. Your ideas are just as important to record as the facts. They will help you process what you are learning, bit by bit. Instead of only recording data, take time to apply your findings to the foundational research questions. The comment section can be divided into three subsections called, "What Happened?" "So What?" and "What Next?" These three questions are helpful for organizing your ideas about filenote information.

What Happened?

Under this heading, comment if something unusual or significant happened during an interview. Unspoken impressions, misunderstandings, or circumstances that affected you or your cultural helper should be described. For example, if your friend held back the truth while her older brother was in the room, but became candid after the brother left, record what happened in this section. You may not have to write about "What Happened" for every filenote. We include this only if it is needed.

So What?

Write an answer to this question for each filenote. How does this interview contribute to your research questions? Why is the information you recorded important? What have you learned about people groups or about how they might be reached with the gospel? In this section, interpret the interview as it applies to church-planting issues.

What Next?

In this final section of the filenote, write down questions you want to ask later. Ideas for future interviews will come to mind as you write each filenote. You might recognize holes in your current research. When you record new questions, you have a quick reminder of them in a handy location. Use these questions to go deeper in later interviews.

Journal Entries

In addition to fieldnotes and filenotes, we keep personal journals of our thoughts and feelings while carrying out research projects (see example, pg. 78). Journal writing has a much different tone than filenote writing and offers many benefits. You can write about struggles and culture stress, vent overwhelming emotions, and thoughtfully explore new ideas, feelings, and experiences. Your journal will contain a wealth of information about the culture and about your experiences as a researcher.

Journal Entry

April 4

Last night we stayed with Maha's family in a village outside of Damascus. Since it's Ramadan, we woke to eat breakfast before sunrise. After eating, we went back to bed while the family washed and got ready to pray. Soon we heard the call to prayer ringing in unmeasured rounds from nearby mosques. I felt guilty for not staying up and praying myself. So many emotions coursed through me as I listened to the call to prayer. It was nearly overwhelming to know that we were the only Christians in this Muslim village, and we are leaving Syria in two months. The alarm clock was ticking loudly, superimposed on the sound of the call to prayer.

In addition to personal journal writing, we keep a team prayer journal. After prayerwalking in the city, we write down highlights of our prayer times: what happened, how we prayed, and spiritual insights we had. You can use this kind of journal writing as research findings as well.

Analysis and Interpretation Notes

Whether you conduct research on your own or as a team, take time to analyze and interpret your findings. Once a week, our teams read each other's filenotes and hold a "strategy meeting" to discuss research findings. One team member takes notes of the conversation. These analysis and interpretation notes record your progression in thinking over time. Even when conducting research alone, analysis and interpretation notes help you recall important ideas. They will also help you write a report for fellow workers, your sending agency, or local church.

Interpreting and Applying Research Findings

After interviewing and making records, you must interpret your findings and apply them to the church planting issues you face. Analysis begins in the "So What?" section of your filenotes, but further work is needed once a collection of filenotes accumulates.

Prayer at dawn in a village outside Damascus.

Five components to effective ethnographic analysis are: 1) examining the information, 2) looking for patterns, 3) looking for alternative interpretations, 4) crystallization, and 5) verification.

Examining the Information

Take time to read and analyze filenotes regularly. If you wait too long, you will be overwhelmed by reading and thinking about everything. On teams of 7-12 researchers who interview three days a week, everyone reads new filenotes once a week. We sit in a group to read filenotes, passing them from one person to the next. Then we hold a group discussion called a strategy meeting. Halfway through a research project, we read all the filenotes again to form a mid-trip summary. Filenotes are also re-read when it is time to compile research findings into a final report. When you read individual filenotes, merge them in your mind so that everything becomes one body of information. Take notes as you read and keep track of your ideas. Parts of the puzzle will begin to come together for you.

Keep your research goals in mind when you read. Review specific goals from the past week or month. Also read with the questions "Who are the peoples?" "What are they like?" and "How can they be reached?" in mind. Read with the end goal in mind – "What might a culturally relevant church look like?" Another set of questions to use while reading is:

- *"What new information has been gathered?"*

- *"What information confirms my ideas?"*

- *"What information contradicts my ideas?"*

Meld raw cultural facts from interviews with your chosen research goals. Specific applications will flow from this convergence.

Looking for Patterns

Answering questions while reading helps you recognize patterns, or cultural themes, that arise from interview information. For example, after a few weeks of research in Bangkok, a pattern emerged in the filenotes regarding the question, "Who are the peoples?" Repeatedly, cultural helpers named the Chinese, the Thai, and the Isaan. A few others also added the Chinese-Thai. Whatever patterns exist and however they apply to church planting will be recognized when reading and analyzing a set of filenotes.

Looking for Alternative Interpretations

As patterns emerge, interpret them. Develop ideas about their meaning. Using the example from Bangkok, you might interpret references to different groups as an indication of people groups. You might postulate that Chinese and Thai people need distinct church-planting efforts. But before you build on these conclusions, look for alternative interpretations. Try to *disprove* your theories. This approach can help you avoid the pitfall of drawing inaccurate conclusions. Again, what information confirms your ideas? What information contradicts your ideas? What else do you still need to investigate? How else might patterns be interpreted, and what else might they mean?

Crystallization

At some point, your thinking will solidify, or crystallize, in your mind. Over time, ideas, applications, and conclusions on many different topics will begin to take shape. Even though you continually face further questions, be patient with yourself in the midst of confusion. *Every* cultural situation is as complex and challenging as the one you are facing! Your ideas, no matter how well founded, are always subject to new information that might make your thinking more accurate.

Verification

The best part about crystallization is that it opens new opportunities to test and verify your ideas with others. Pray specifically about them and ask for spiritual discernment. Your cultural helpers are a great asset at this time. Ask them what they think about your conclusions. Their input usually sharpens or deepens conclusions you are forming. Include the experience and perspective of national believers and other Christian workers in the verification process.

Setting New Directions

Each period of analysis and interpretation is a time to set new directions for your research. A wide variety of unresolved questions are usually available to choose from! Try to narrow the topics you want to investigate next. Choose new topics on the basis of your research goals, and not merely on your curiosity about interesting side issues.

Keep focused! Ask yourself how you are doing in regard to the big picture. Have you spent sufficient time on each broad research question: Who are the peoples? What are they like? How can they be reached? Have you emphasized one area of interest over another? If so, choose new research goals to balance and broaden your perspective. Have you exhausted a particular research topic or do you need to flesh things out more? For example, you may feel that you have asked sufficient questions about neighborhoods and leadership, but that you are inadequately informed about religion and folk practices. If so, drop neighborhood and leadership topics and focus on religion.

A key to setting new research directions is moving on when you need to, yet staying focused for sufficient lengths of time. Consider the pace you want to keep. At the same time, recognize the holes that remain in your research.

Writing a Report

Writing a report is often the final step in an ethnographic study. This report serves the purpose for which your studies have been done. We have used research findings to write a variety of materials such as prayer guide booklets and scripts for videos. These "final reports" have primarily had a motivational purpose. We have also written summaries for missionary field conferences addressing current church-planting issues. Strategy reports have been written for mission executives, new missionary recruits, and for missionaries and national workers. Final reports usually emphasize cultural description, make applications to church-planting issues, and occasionally call for specific action to be taken (see Appendix II for a list of Caleb Project mobilization tools which have been created based on our research).

Remember Your Audience

The kind of writing you do depends entirely upon the audience you hope to address. A thesis committee or a university professor is a different audience than a local church or a mission agency. As you design your research project, and certainly before you begin writing, ask "Who will read and use these materials?" What is your audience like and how can you approach them effectively?

Choose a form

Just as audiences differ, forms of writing differ. A Ph.D. thesis is written differently than a prayer guide. Decide on a format for your writing that is appropriate for your audience. Length, style, and content depend on your choice. Consider the final format. Will you produce a book, a booklet, a flyer or handout, a paper, or a letter? Will you include pictures or diagrams, or use other communication devices?

Design the piece of writing

After selecting your audience and form, your writing should be directed by a design. Decide what you want to say. Make a list of topics that you want to include, and then create an outline of how you might arrange the parts or sections of writing. Your arrangement should benefit the reader, building one idea upon another so that others understand what you are saying.

Write a draft

Once you settle on an outline that you feel accomplishes your writing goals, begin composing each section. A timeline and checklist for yourself or for your team will help set an effective pace for completing your project.

Use examples from filenotes as often as possible. Filenotes and journal entries are particularly helpful in writing descriptive sections. Use plenty of examples. Turn your filenotes into stories about the people you have met. A story or vignette may be based on one person and their family, or it may be a combination of many stories into one accurate, but fictitious illustration. Use important native terms and quotes to interest your readers.

Depending on the final length, writing a first draft can take a great deal of time and effort. As with the research itself, stay focused! Communicate clearly using topic sentences and complete paragraphs. The more accurately you define your topic in each section, the less confusion and effort writing will take.

Editing

Once you complete an entire rough draft, take a break! You not only deserve it, your editing will be more effective and ruthless if you have a few days' breather. Step back and see whether what you have written communicates everything that you hoped it would. Are there significant facets of the culture that have not been represented? Looking back at filenotes, journal entries, and analysis and interpretation notes at this point is helpful. Re-read them, and if needed, revise the outline and expand your first draft to include pertinent information.

Editing is a *necessary* part of producing a final written piece. Re-read the draft yourself, and recruit a few outside readers. Their perspective can be extremely helpful. Look for and find things you have taken for granted. What seems unclear? What has been misunderstood and why? What questions do other readers have? Combine editing suggestions with your own ideas and incorporate them into a final draft. Then write an introduction and conclusion that fits the piece and aids the reader.

Printing and Publication

Producing a piece in quantity may require the services of a printer and graphic artist. Work with the final text to design and create a printed piece that meets your specific goals. Appendix II includes a list of various publications we have created based on our research. They may spark new ideas about using research to communicate to a variety of people.

Conclusion

An effective research project has many steps and requires new skills. Remember, the task is not impossible! Simply live life with unreached people, keep track of what you learn, and put your mind to work. Part III will make your task even more do-able, giving you specific topics of interest to pursue.

Part III:
Going To Work

Our fieldwork in urban settings has evolved. Along the way, more questions have been raised than answered about discovering ways for unreached people to follow Christ. But God has gone with us. What we have learned can give direction to others who share a passion for the lost and a heart for church planting.

Without direction, you could easily spend years collecting more and more information. All cultures are incredibly fascinating and each one is unique. What specific information do you really want to gather? With limited time and resources, you must go to work with a pointed research focus. "Who are the peoples?" "What are they like?" and "How can they be reached?" are questions that provide a starting point and a plumb line for fieldwork. Now that you are acquainted with ethnographic skills and the research process, these questions can be fleshed out. Part III describes in detail the areas of interest we investigate to more fully address these three research questions.

A Menu of Research Topics

Once a Caleb Project Research Expedition has been designed and researchers arrive overseas, they apply a menu of research topics to their urban situation. These topics are particularly interesting to us because of our focus on church planting. Research topics are grouped into four specific areas of interest: social stratification, social structure, social dynamics, and evangelization. Each area contains a variety of topics for investigation.

Introducing the Areas of Interest

Social Stratification

Social stratification helps you discover the outlines of significant population segments and leads you to an understanding of people groups in your city. Pursuing social stratification helps you speak knowledgeably about people groups and make wise church-planting decisions based on that understanding.

Social Structure

Once a working knowledge of social stratification is underway, you can expand your understanding of any people group by studying social structure. Whereas stratification reveals boundaries between groups, social structure reveals how people relate to others. People groups are more than a collection of disconnected individuals; they are composed of people who are connected to one another and to outsiders. Topics explored within social structure include relationship networks, kinship and family, associations and institutions, and leadership.

Social Dynamics

Like social structure, social dynamics interest us because they help us understand what particular people groups are like. Certain forces push, shape, and mold the social evolution of every culture. People groups are not static. You need to see where a society is coming from and, more importantly, where it may be going. Topics included in the study of social dynamics are urbanization, modernization, religion, education, government policy and economics, communication, history, and demographics.

Evangelization

The fourth area of interest explores the presence of Christianity among particular people groups both in history and at present. Topics included in this category are history of evangelization, church growth, and receptivity.

Who's Who in the Zoo: Social Stratification

When you enter an unreached urban setting, begin with stratification studies. You want to put together a good overall picture of the different kinds of groups represented in your city. People always have their own, familiar ways to group, classify, categorize, peg, pigeonhole, and distinguish each other.

Begin by asking yourself broad questions such as:

- *What boundaries exist between people in this city and culture? What is their significance for church planting?*

- *How many church planting efforts are needed in this city?*

- *If ten missionaries could be deployed at once, where should they focus their efforts to maximize the spread of the gospel through as many segments of the population as possible?*

More specifically, you want to evaluate the groups you discover to discern whether or not they are people groups. To understand where one people group ends and the next begins, we evaluate society according to two criteria. They are social identity and group allegiance. These criteria help answer the question, "Is this group of people actually a people group?" In combination, identity and allegiance give solid indication of people group distinctions.

Criteria One: Social Identity

Social identity is a sense of group uniqueness based on similarity to one another and distinction from others. Social identity occurs in a collection of people when they perceive that, "We are us because of this." "This" is often a combination of many factors such as a common ethnic heritage, a shared history or language, a common station in life, or a particular brand of religion. Discerning people group researchers ask, "To what degree does this group see itself as distinct within society?"

A sense of social identity can vary from one group to another. For example, Uzbek villagers in Uzbekistan have a strong sense of social identity. These villagers often say, "We are traditional (or 'real') Uzbeks. We keep Uzbek traditions and we are not like modern Uzbeks."

On the other hand, a group's sense of social identity can be weak. Such groups see themselves as common – blending easily with others in the society. In this case the group is probably only a sub-set of a larger collection of people and not a people group itself. For example, in Malaysia various groups of Malay include Kampung Malay, Old-Money Malay, and Progressive Malay. These groups, however, do not see themselves as very distinct from one another. Each of the three groups' sense of social identity is weak. They share a more significant social identity as *Malay*.

Diagram 4

Degrees of Social Identity
"To what degree does a group see itself as distinct within society?"

Common   Distinct

| *No unique identity. "We are like everyone else."* | *No group name but some sense of social identity. "We are like most others."* | *Group name and stronger sense of social identity. "Most others are not like us."* | *Distinct identity. "We are a group, and others are not a part of us."* |

Diagram 5

Degrees of Group Allegiance

"To what degree do group members see themselves as being connected to one another through influential relationships?"

Fluid Relationships	Elastic Relationships	Stiff Relationships	Brittle Relationships
Member's relationships provide no meaningful sense of connection to the group and do not influence personal and lifestyle decisions.	*Some sense of connection. Group members, perhaps only a few friends, influence decisions.*	*Significant sense of connection. Group members, such as immediate family and friends, influence decisions.*	*Relationships provide all of one's connection to the group. Extended and immediate family, friends and neighbors, influence all personal and lifestyle decisions.*

Criteria Two: Group Allegiance

Social identity is not enough to define people groups in the complexity of urban life. Sets of people in many cities around the world share a common identity but lack cohesion. Thus, a second factor must be considered when you are determining people groups.

Groups significant for church planting will not only have a strong sense of social identity but will also stick together with a sense of connection to one another. Relationships will be characterized by loyalty to others within the group who influence personal and lifestyle decisions. This sense of connection through relationships is known as group allegiance (see Diagram 5).

Discerning people group researchers ask, "To what degree do group members see themselves as connected to one another through influential relationships?" A set of people cannot be considered a people group unless they are bound together by networks of relationships. In addition, the more rigid relationship networks are, the more likely that people group dynamics will profoundly affect the work of church planting.

The Test of Strength: Boundary Maintenance

The strength of a group's identity and allegiance can be seen most clearly by the thickness of the walls they build between themselves and other groups. This wall

High boundary maintenance and enduring group identity indicate a people group significant for church planting.

building, called boundary maintenance, describes the tendency of groups to restrict interaction with members of other groups. Boundaries are maintained by societal limitation on whom one can marry, befriend, and even do business with. Strong boundary maintenance will limit the flow of the gospel from one group to another. Whenever a group exhibits high boundary maintenance, it is likely to be a people group.

The Test of Time: Durability

Another test of people groupness is durability, that is, a group's identity and allegiance must remain over time. University students are therefore not a people group. We would not envision a special cluster of churches of, by, and for university students because within a five-year period, they would no longer share that identity. Groups of people in which grandparents and their grandchildren share the same fundamental identity are more likely to be a people group.

Likewise, a true people group's identity should remain intact after repentance. Therefore, we would not see "prostitutes of San Francisco" as a people group for pioneer church planting because the gospel would dissolve the distinctive feature of their association. Such groups may require specialized evangelistic approaches, but not their own church-planting movement.

Three Research Activities

Three research activities produce results in the area of social stratification. They are building taxonomies, describing groups, and ascertaining boundaries. These activities are accomplished by thoughtfully considering interview information. In his book, *The Ethnographic Interview*, James P. Spradley presents additional concepts such as taxonomic analysis, cover terms, and domain and componential analysis. We have made vigorous use of these concepts. You too can understand and use these tools to supplement your work, even though you might be a novice.

Building Taxonomies

Make taxonomies of groups of people as your first step in interpreting your research. A taxonomy is a list of all the kinds of something and their relationship to one another. For example, you could list all ethnic groups, or all religious sects, or all language groups that cultural helpers mention. The most prized taxonomies contain ideas that people hold about themselves and others. Learn *their* categories of description. It is essential that you do not superimpose your own ideas. For example, in an early interview with a cultural helper, you might ask a grand tour question like, "Who lives in this city?" This is a good beginning question compared to a poor question like, "What kinds of religious groups are there?" This question is poor because you assume that your helper thinks in religious terms. Religion is *your* category, not theirs. Your cultural helper might not have spoken of religious groupings as a significant distinguishing factor had you not suggested that category. Find out the terms, names, and the classifications of as many groups as you can. Try to understand these groups just as they are described to you. Who is grouped together with whom and by whom?

Some common ways that different cultures segment themselves are listed in Table 6. Remember, various cultures define social stratification by different characteristics. Use *their* ideas. For example, in India, cultural helpers speak of caste and religious fervor as distinguishing characteristics, whereas urban Thai people speak of occupational and ethnic groupings.

Once you develop taxonomies, examine them according to the criteria of a people group. Remember, a people group is the largest group within which the gospel can spread as a church-planting movement without encountering barriers of understanding or acceptance. Do some identities merge into larger, more comprehensive groups through which the gospel can spread? What barriers of understanding and acceptance truly divide people into people groups?

Table 6 Possible Research Topics for Stratification			
CLS	Class brackets	STS	Status, Role, Prestige, Name
ETH	Ethnicity	POL	Political parties
LNG	Language and dialects	CST	Caste or tribal groups
NBR	Neighborhoods	REO	Region of origin
OCC	Occupations	SEC	Degree of secularization
RLB	Religious beliefs	MOD	Degree of modernization
EDC	Education	MIG	Stage of migration

After one month of interviewing Muslims in Bombay, a research team reviewed their filenotes to prepare for a strategy meeting. As they read, they collected their ideas regarding stratification. Then they developed the taxonomy shown below.

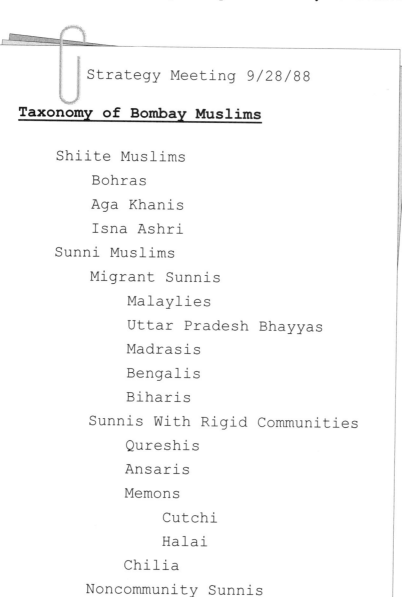

Strategy Meeting 9/28/88

Taxonomy of Bombay Muslims

Shiite Muslims
    Bohras
    Aga Khanis
    Isna Ashri
Sunni Muslims
    Migrant Sunnis
        Malaylies
        Uttar Pradesh Bhayyas
        Madrasis
        Bengalis
        Biharis
    Sunnis With Rigid Communities
        Qureshis
        Ansaris
        Memons
            Cutchi
            Halai
        Chilia
    Noncommunity Sunnis

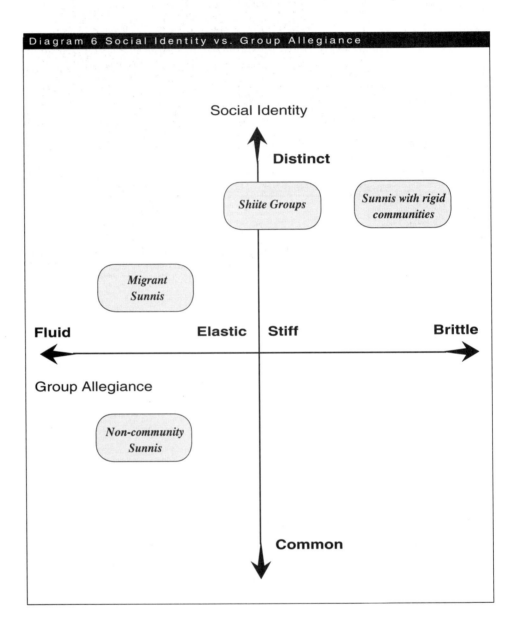

Diagram 6 Social Identity vs. Group Allegiance

The team in Bombay analyzed their taxonomy by plotting groups of people according to degree of social identity and group allegiance. Groups of people display their sense of identity and allegiance to different degrees. The results are shown above. The research team concluded:

"Bombay's Muslims form a complex mosaic. One and a half million people are divided into several groups based on a variety of factors such as religious sect, region of origin, migration, socio-economic status, and occupation. The most basic division is between Shiite and Sunni Muslims. This is the most important internal divider for the Muslims of Bombay. Within each group there are further divisions based on factors mentioned above."

If you notice a group of women in unusual dress ask, "Those ladies dress differently. Can you tell me about them?"

Describing Groups

Building taxonomies is one stratification activity. The second is describing groups you have identified. Both activities are not difficult to combine. As you learn how people view themselves and others in their city, you also collect valuable descriptive information. As soon as you use categories and terms that people easily recognize, you can learn more directly about the different groups.

Interview cultural helpers in these ways:

- *Ask to hear true stories about a group, from both insiders and outsiders. For example, ask your friend who is a Bohra to tell you the history of his people. What do they have in common? What are important characteristics of Bohras? Ask a Sunni Muslim if she has any Bohra friends. If not, why not? What do Sunnis think about Bohras?*

- *Ask about distinctive symbols which mark or identify members of a particular group. For example, you may be walking down the street with your cultural helper. If you notice a group of women in unusual dress ask, "Those ladies dress differently. Can you tell me about them?" Or you may ask, "How can I tell the difference between a Bihari and an Ansari?"*

- *Ask projective questions, contrasting behavior of different groups. For example, "If I were to attend an Aga Khani wedding, how would it differ from a Memon wedding?"*

- *Ask to meet or observe some people from a particular group. To a good cultural helper you might say, "I have heard that Sunnis and Shias in Bombay have different mosques. Could you take me to visit both places?"*

- *Watch social scenes and become proficient in identifying different groups.*

- *Watch the interactions between members of different groups, if there are any points of contact.*

- *Watch for the use of distinctive language by various groups.*

When you gather descriptive information, maintain a fascination for each group and for the mundane aspects of their lives. You might tend to highlight exceptional events, the boldest of contrasts, and the rarely performed rituals that distinguish a particular group. Aim to describe *basic* daily behavior of groups of people. Pick up information about nondescript, day-to-day characteristics as well as special occasions and distinctive features.

Ascertaining Boundaries

The third research activity that is involved in stratification studies is ascertaining group boundaries. Many social boundaries are not absolute barriers preventing all social interaction. A scale exists, and somewhere along that scale, boundaries become impermeable enough to be important to the work of planting churches.

Keep track of how people identify each other, or what symbols signal someone's identity. The symbols in other cultures are sometimes garish to the foreign eye. At other times, they are so subtle that we are unable to detect them on our own. For example, the team in Bombay noticed right away that in a nearby neighborhood, many of the women were wearing bright *bourkas* (a covering worn by some Indian Muslim women) of a particular style. Upon questioning, they learned that these particular *bourkas* represented the compulsory *rida* dress of the Bohra Muslim women. This is just one example of an easily recognized symbol of identity. Often, symbols of identity are more hidden. For example, in Japan, businessmen always exchange their company cards when they are introduced to each other. To an American, this custom would appear to be a mere convenience – something that would help one businessman contact another at a later date. Further investigation reveals that exchanging business cards in Japan has tremendous significance in terms of one's identity and status. It is like handing another person a complete set of rules concerning subsequent social interactions. Business cards in Japan are crucial to an understanding of boundary maintenance, but only a Japanese person could describe the meaning and significance to an outsider.

Attitudes are often attached to symbols of identity and contribute to boundary maintenance between groups of people. For example, whenever we mentioned the Shamee of Damascus to other groups of people in the city, they commented about that group's wealth and power. Such attitudes feed a system of boundary maintenance. Attitudes like respect, disgust, deference, servitude, impatience, or gratitude may fuel daily interactions between people of different groups.

Explore the reasons behind attitudes that people have toward one another. Listen carefully to religious or historical explanations for the way people feel. Sometimes, as in India, boundaries between groups are maintained according to religious beliefs regarding cleanness or purity. Strict rules are maintained to "protect" high castes from being defiled by low castes.

Fatima: Seeking Salvation

Fatima is one of the 50,000 Bohras of Bombay who are caught in an intricate web of untruth. Daily she strives to lead a life worthy of salvation. She wears the compulsory rida *dress of the Bohra women and prays three times a day. Fatima's dress is a symbol indicating boundarires between her people and others.*

Some areas to consider when investigating boundary maintenance include:

- *Inter-marriage: "Would you let your daughter marry a Zulu?"*

- *Receiving food or drink for ceremonial or sustenance purposes: "If you were hungry, would you eat in the home of a Masai?"*

- *Returning or giving a greeting: "How do you know to bow to someone before greeting them?"*

- *Participating together in religious ceremonies: (To an Uzbek) "Who will be invited to your son's circumcision party? Will your Russian neighbor attend?"*

- *Using the same transportation: "Why aren't there veiled women on the bus? How do they go from place to place?"*

"As a Shamee, would you ever consider going into business with someone from the village? What is important in making such a decision?"

- *Making business deals with others: "As a Shamee, would you ever consider going into business with someone from the village? What is important in making such a decision?"*

- *Forming friendships with each other: "Who are your best friends at the university?"*

- *Visiting or entering homes, neighborhoods, or other areas: "Have you ever visited the Palestinian camp? What was it like?"*

- *Sharing the same occupation with the same remunerations: "What jobs do Chinese prefer, in comparison to the Malay?"*

The following example of research as it was carried out in Damascus briefly illustrates a team's stratification studies. This example was written by the team's research coordinator (see Part IV for an explanation of the research coordinator's role on a team).

Before going to Syria, each team member read a few general articles on the peoples of Syria. These articles seemed to indicate the presence of a wide variety of ethnic groups, especially in the capital city of Damascus. The following dynamics seemed to be at work: an oppressive government, political instability, and migration to the city. Also, people who had visited Damascus told us that Islamic practice was very high.

During the first few weeks in Damascus, we focused our studies on stratification. Who was represented in the city? What people groups were there? How many church-planting efforts would be needed for the gospel to spread throughout the entire city?

I sent half of the team members to the university to meet English speakers and the other half took buses to check out the perimeters of the city. How big was Damascus? How many different areas were there? Once cultural helpers were found, each teamlet pursued stratification studies using the topics of region of origin, migration, ethnicity, language, and neighborhood.

After a month of interviewing, notetaking, and strategy meetings, we found ourselves in a maze of groups of people. We had identified large groups like Villagers, Golanese, Shamee, and Palestinians, as well as small groups like Christians of various types, Kurds, Druze, Jews, Cherkess, and Adygei. Due to limited time (three months, and one month was already past) we decided to focus on three Muslim groups: the Shamee, the Kurds, and the Palestinians.

These groups maintained boundaries between each other. Shamee defined themselves by their ancient ties to the city and by the distinct communities in which they lived. We observed that the Shamee occupied an exclusive social and economic niche.

The Kurds in Damascus were recent migrants from villages. They spoke Kirmanji rather than Arabic, and resented the government's attempts to Arabize them. Most lived on the outskirts of the city. Those who lived farther out had assimilated even less than those who lived closer in. Recent migrants were also less assimilated than those who had lived in the city for a longer time.

The Palestinians, though they shared many characteristics with other Arabs, seemed to be another unique group in Damascus. Many first settled in refugee camps in the city. Over the years their camps had been transformed into functional communities. These distinct neighborhoods helped maintain Palestinian identity – effectively separating Palestinians from others. We felt that unique church-planting efforts were needed to reach the Shamee, Kurds, and Palestinians with the gospel.

Once their focus became limited, the team in Damascus was ready to delve deeper into the questions, "What are they like?" and "How can they be reached?"

The Warp and Woof: Social Structure

Stratification studies help define barriers between groups but social structure helps us understand significant relationships within groups. Social structure is about how people groups relate among themselves and with others. This area of interest is important to church planting because it clarifies people group distinctions. It also gives insight into how the gospel might naturally spread through the relationships which make up the fabric of a society. What is the warp and woof of the people? What holds them together? How do they relate to one another?

Relationship networks have been referred to as the "bridges of God."

Four new research topics will be introduced in this section: relationship networks, kinship and family ties, associations and institutions, and leadership. Other topics may also contribute to social structure, but the ones described here seem to apply in every urban situation.

Relationship Networks

Understanding interpersonal relationships within a societal group leads to insights regarding the bonds that tie a people group together. Bonds exist between your cultural helper and everyone with whom they relate. These bonds form relationship webs called "networks." Relationship networks have been referred to as the "bridges of God" within a people group by the missiologist Dr. Donald MacGavran. Through such relationships the gospel message will likely be shared from one person to another.

In *Anthropology of the City,* Edwin Eames and Judith Granich Goode introduce relationship networks in the urban context. They write,

Underlying the network concept is the assumption that individuals in complex, urban social systems are faced with a large range of potential social relationships. Rather than acting largely as a member of ascribed kin groups, the individual selects *from this potential range those with whom he or she will establish social ties. Such networks are* egocentric *– in the sense that a particular individual selects those with whom he will establish bonds of intimacy and mutual obligation. Thus, no two individuals will have exactly the same social network.*

When cultural helpers establish social ties with others, they reveal a great deal about themselves and about how relationships work. For example, how are life-long friendships formed and how or when do they begin? Or, with whom does your cultural helper trade at the local market?

While it is true that no two individuals within a people group have exactly the same social networks, recurring themes emerge among social networks. These themes may highlight or confirm boundaries between people groups. For example, if true Thai people rarely form relationships with Chinese people, how will the gospel spread from one group to another? In this sense, network analysis is useful for stratification studies.

Other themes emerge that reveal how people relate to one another, make decisions together, and influence one another's lives. This information specifically highlights social structure. Social structure helps a missionary consider what it means to plant churches that fit the natural grain or pattern of a people group. Fellowships that go with the social grain will not needlessly resist the culture or extract new believers from their friends and family. When churches fit social

Fellowships that go with the social grain will not needlessly extract new believers from their friends and family.

structure patterns, barriers of understanding and acceptance can be reduced to only those which remain because of the offense of the gospel.

Before you study relationship networks, compile some information about people groups and establish trusting relationships with a few cultural helpers. If these first steps are omitted, it will be much harder to integrate, interpret, and analyze network information. Specifically, begin network analysis once you have a general understanding about how families and friendships work. Know native terms for different groups of people, kinds of friends, and family members. It is helpful (but not necessary) to be acquainted with a group of friends who know each other well and to have participated in some activity together with them.

To study relationship networks, begin asking questions like these:

- *Who do you see daily/weekly/monthly?*

- *Who are your friends/neighbors/colleagues/fellow caste members? Could you name a few and describe them to me?*

Drawing network diagrams with your cultural helper can be a lot of fun.

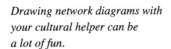

- *Who calls on you for help in difficult times? Whom do you call for help? What kind of help might you/they give?*

- *Who do you trust/believe/tell your secrets to?*

- *Who influences the direction of your life or the decisions you make?*

- *Who is the most trusted/respected/ listened to person among your friends? In your community? Why do you listen to what they say?*

Getting acquainted with just one social network will flood your mind with information, ideas, and cultural insight. What you learn can be difficult to record, just because there is so much to learn. Use simple diagrams to gather network information. These diagrams depict the members of a particular network and their relationships with each other. Work with your cultural helper to make a network diagram. Record your cultural helper's explanations along with your own thoughts. Drawing network diagrams with cultural helpers can be a lot of fun.

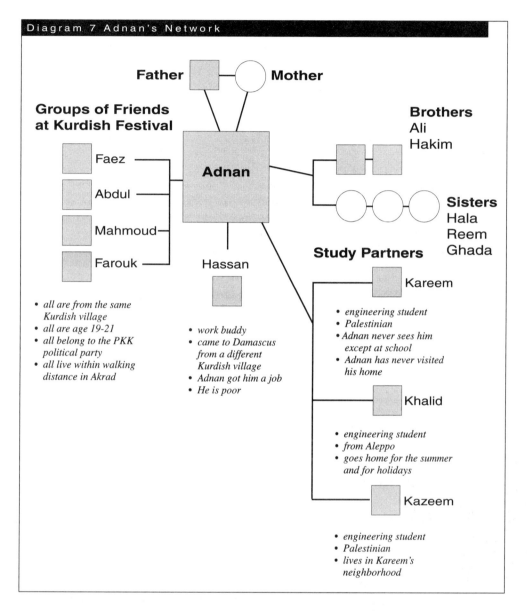

Diagram 7 Adnan's Network

Father ☐ ─ ○ **Mother**

Groups of Friends at Kurdish Festival

☐ Faez ─

☐ Abdul ─

☐ Mahmoud ─

☐ Farouk ─

Adnan

Brothers
Ali
Hakim

Sisters
Hala
Reem
Ghada

Hassan

- *all are from the same Kurdish village*
- *all are age 19-21*
- *all belong to the PKK political party*
- *all live within walking distance in Akrad*

- *work buddy*
- *came to Damascus from a different Kurdish village*
- *Adnan got him a job*
- *He is poor*

Study Partners

☐ Kareem

- *engineering student*
- *Palestinian*
- *Adnan never sees him except at school*
- *Adnan has never visited his home*

☐ Khalid

- *engineering student*
- *from Aleppo*
- *goes home for the summer and for holidays*

☐ Kazeem

- *engineering student*
- *Palestinian*
- *lives in Kareem's neighborhood*

Ours have often insisted on helping us, and they have added corrections that we forgot or didn't yet know. Later, diagrams will help tremendously in drawing conclusions and identifying themes.

The center of Diagram 7 represents a cultural helper, "Adnan," whom we interviewed. Surrounding him are other circles (females) and squares (males) who represent the people Adnan relates to on a regular basis. Notes have been added to help compare one network to another and to show information about Adnan's relationships. If necessary, different lines could have been used to connect the squares and circles. They can be keyed to indicate degree of intimacy, blood ties, or any other relevant information.

Once you have developed useful network diagrams and asked questions about them, move on to analyze what you have learned. To analyze your diagrams and interview information, take particular note of the qualities of intimacy and influence, complexity, density, elasticity, and durability.

Network Analysis

Intimacy and Influence

Rank relationships in a person's network according to varying degrees of intimacy and influence. Intimacy can be gauged according to different relational dynamics. For example, Americans typically measure intimacy by the freedom we feel to share personal matters with someone else. But in other cultures intimacy may be measured very differently – perhaps according to respect, years of knowing a person, or knowing the family background of a friend.

While intimacy is associated with the amount of sharing between individuals, influence indicates who wields authority and who has power in decision making. Levels of intimacy may indicate who wields influence and how they do so.

Some people are mere acquaintances while others are daily companions who are sought out, loved, and honored continually. Still others can be contacted only when needed to help achieve a goal or solve a problem. The former network is called the effective or intimate network. The latter is called the extended or instrumental network. Both kinds of networks are important for different reasons.

In most cases, the gospel travels well between people who have intimate relationships with each other. Identifying intimate bonds may reveal ways that the gospel could spread easily and naturally within a network. Network information may lead to insights regarding ways that missionaries would want to get involved and form friendships within a particular people group. On the other hand, if intimate relationships are of little influence, the gospel might be stopped by others of influence who might oppose it. Sometimes tremendous pressure is exerted by the instrumental network. This pressure will need to be considered.

Complexity

Some relationships are multi-dimensional in that individuals often relate to the same people in different ways at different times. For example, the relationship between two players on a soccer team who only see each other at the field once a week is not a complex one. But if the two soccer players are cousins who attend the same school and who are taught Islam by the same *mullah* in a neighborhood where they both live, then the relationship is complex. If people in a network relate to each other in more than one role, then those relationships may offer deeper intimacy and greater influence.

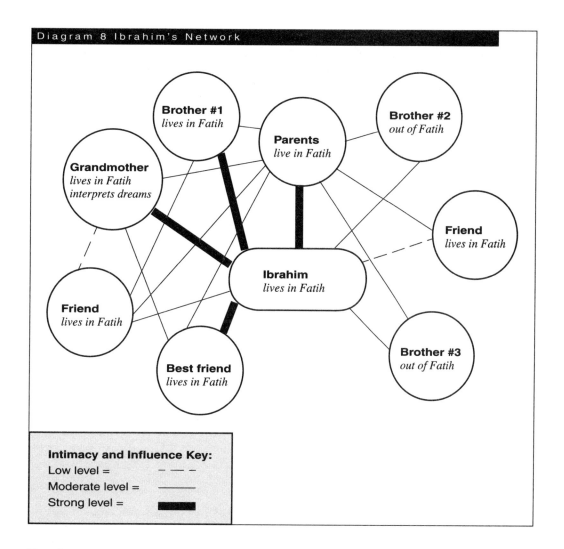

Diagram 8 Ibrahim's Network

Intimacy and Influence Key:
Low level = – — –
Moderate level = ———
Strong level = ▬▬▬

Density

After identifying the people in your cultural helper's social network, it is important to find out how these various people are related to one another. In some cases, your cultural helper will know everyone, but few of those people, if any, will know one another. In other cases, everyone will know everyone else, and this is considered a "high-density" network. The more dense a network is, the more advisable it is to include all of the network in an evangelistic strategy. Also, if an individual's network has almost no density, find out if this is common to most within this particular people group. If not, your friend may be on the fringe of society, and may not represent others in his or her people group well.

Diagram 8 shows Ibrahim's network. This network is a good example of the concepts used in network analysis. Ibrahim is a Turk who lives in Fatih, a completely Turkish neighborhood. The diagram of Ibrahim's network has been drawn to illustrate aspects of intimacy and influence. Dotted lines indicate low

Ibrahim and his grandmother.

levels, thin lines indicate moderate levels, and thick lines indicate very strong levels of intimacy and influence. These designations were made based on interview information and are not complete.

Ibrahim's network is somewhat *complex* in that his grandmother fills more than one role in Ibrahim's life. She is his relative, she lives next door as a neighbor, two of his best friends know her well, and she is also a renowned interpreter of dreams in the neighborhood.

Ibrahim's network is *dense* in that almost all of the people he relates to know each other. Except for his two oldest brothers, Ibrahim's family and friends all live in the neighborhood of Fatih.

Elasticity

Perhaps the most important and intricate dynamic of networks is their degree of elasticity. Elasticity refers to the responses of people within a network to aberrant behavior. In other words, how resilient are relationships within the network? How much deviant behavior will be tolerated before relationships are severed?

In Bombay, a few Bohras were asked how their family and friends would react if they decided to change religions. One young boy said his parents wouldn't let him change his religion and he wouldn't want to. He said, "I am proud to be a Bohra." When the issue was pressed a bit further he said, "If I changed my religion, my parents would throw me out of the house!" Another cultural helper, when asked how the community would respond to a Bohra changing his religion said that, by order of the *Syedna* (or religious leader), the members of the community would not be allowed to communicate or associate with that person.

In general, the elasticity of a network can be ranked according to a scale ranging from fluid to elastic to stiff to brittle. Fluid networks tolerate almost anything. Brittle networks break with objectionable behavior. The examples given above from the Bohra community illustrate brittle networks – aberrant behavior might result in the termination of a relationship or at least a substantial loss of intimacy and respect.

Estimating elasticity helps us anticipate how people might respond to an individual who begins to follow Christ. To the degree that conversion is viewed as aberrant behavior, we can predict the relational loss that a new convert might experience. For example, in some Muslim communities, a change of religion is behavior worthy of death. Among some Buddhists, a convert may be mocked and suffer social ostracism from some people but will be able to carry on a fairly normal life with others.

If we have an idea about what will happen to someone who decides to follow Christ, we can plan and pray accordingly. Perhaps some evangelistic strategies can limit the social ostracism of a new convert. By taking into account the flow of relationships, missionaries and budding fellowships might protect and use existing networks as avenues through which the gospel can be shared.

Durability

Durability refers to the life span of a particular network, and it is also a factor to recognize when analyzing network diagrams. The durability of a network can be difficult to determine, but fairly accurate ideas can be formed by gathering stories of how long-lived certain kinds of relationships may be, or by asking questions which reveal your cultural helper's expectations for various relationships.

The most valuable network information comes from analyzing information from a variety of network diagrams. Reliable conclusions can be made by comparing many network diagrams and records. Look for themes or striking contrasts between relationships that different kinds of people have.

Kinship and Family Ties

The topic of kinship and family ties is a specialized topic within relationship networks. This topic focuses on relationships and their meaning among family members. It does not include other important people such as friends, teachers, and business associates who are not related to your cultural helper by blood ties.

A Kurdish Church?

I went to Kamar's house for lunch one day. She and her family are Kurdish. Our conversation turned to spiritual things when I asked Kamar what might happen if a Kurd became a Christian. She told me that really, she had never heard of such a thing. In the Qur'an, *it says that you must kill any person who leaves Islam. I told her I thought a family must love too much to kill, even if someone left Islam. She was quiet for a moment. Then she told me about the "Islam government" in Damascus.*

There are leaders who, if they heard of a Kurd becoming a Christian, would come to the house and talk to the person and beat them. They have the responsibility to kill any converts. I wondered how any Kurdish Christian could ever tell anyone they had left Islam for Christ.

When I left Kamar's house in the late afternoon, a lot of questions were spinning in my head. If a Kurd ever became a Christian, how could they follow Christ and withstand the persecution? Could the first converts wait to tell their family until there was a whole group of Kurdish believers to support them? What if the Kurdish church celebrated Christ in Kurdish ways? Probably the most churning issue in my heart was that Kamar had said she'd never heard of a Kurd becoming a Christian. Will the Kurdish people hear of Jesus soon?

Carol McKinney, an associate professor at the Graduate Institute of Applied Linguistics in Texas, has written a book that describes how to carry out in-depth studies of kinship, marriage, descent, and residence, as well as on how to collect life histories. Her book, *Globe Trotting in Sandals: Culture Research Field Methods Guide* is a helpful book to supplement your work.

Family relationships are usually the most personal and intimate of all relationships. Overall objectives to keep in mind when focusing on this topic include:

> **Note**
>
> *Sometimes cultural helpers call many people by the same name. For example, Arab men often call all their cousins and sometimes their neighborhood friends "brother." When gathering family information, ask questions like, "Who are your mother's sons?" rather than "Who are your brothers?"*

- *Gathering terms of reference and ways of addressing kin*

- *Identifying and describing family values and ideas of honor*

- *Learning about marriage patterns, customs, and values*

- *Learning about decision making within the family context*

- *Exploring different family forms, typical domestic units, and extended families*

- *Gathering life histories and family stories.*

Three approaches to studying kinship and family ties can be taken. These include creating a family "tree," noting family styles, and examining family operations.

Family relationships are usually the most personal and intimate of all relationships.

Family Trees

Family trees are diagrams that depict family members from more than one generation. They are a means of charting kinship relationships. Many conversations and interviews might be needed to learn enough about one particular family in order to create a family tree. However, the rewards of learning in this fashion can be great. Family trees lead to understanding kinship systems, patterns, and ways of thinking that set cultural "rules" for functioning as a family in a particular society.

Indonesian kampung.

Two examples illustrate the richness of charting family and kinship relationships. In Indonesia, one research team decided to chart kinship relationships in the neighborhood in which they lived. The neighborhood, called the *kampung*, appeared to be very close-knit. Starting with an elderly woman in the *kampung*, the team charted kinship relationships and discovered strategic insights. First, they learned that the *kampung* is matrilocal. That is, most of the women of a family remain in their neighborhood of birth; the men come from other *kampungs*.

Second, the team discovered that 75% of the people in their *kampung* were related by blood ties. They were descendents of two powerful grandmothers of the *kampung*. Perhaps the most important finding of the team's entire research was an understanding of the *kampung* and its role in this people group's social structure. Many of the team's ideas for effective church planting flowed from their insight regarding family relationships in the *kampung*.

Another example comes from studies done among the Turkmen of Ashgabat, Turkmenistan. When the team asked about the family trees of their cultural helpers, they discovered that many lost grandparents in a devastating earthquake in 1948. Many orphans were adopted into relatives' households after the calamity. This information, combined with a growing understanding of the role that Soviet Communism played over the past 70 years, explained why young Turkmen were unable to articulate the story of their people. It also explained their confusion over Turkmen culture and identity. Few surviving grandparents remain today in Ashgabat to pass on the legacy of what it really means to be Turkmen.

Family Styles

Many different family styles exist, and they can be even more complex in urban settings. Studying individual households or domestic groups is the easiest way to pursue an understanding of family styles. Eames and Goode define a domestic group as "individuals who pool economic resources and cooperate in the performance of domestic activities: shopping, cooking, eating, cleaning, laundry, and child care."

Typical domestic groups for a particular people group may or may not correspond to western-style nuclear families of father, mother, and siblings. For example, in Damascus, the Shamee live in two kinds of groups. Some live in neighborhoods called *muhallas*. Here, characteristic Arab homes house as many as thirty family members in an extended family household. Other Shamee live outside *muhallas* in apartments as nuclear families. However, the flats in an entire apartment building are commonly occupied by brothers, cousins, and their wives and children. In reality, the extended family atmosphere of the *muhalla* is preserved in the apartment building. The preferred family style of the Shamee is the extended family style – in any workable form.

Migration and urban occupations can also force some interesting household patterns. The joint family is an amalgamation of individuals or nuclear families who have recently migrated to the city where they live and work together. In New Delhi, India many of the newly established *bastis*, or slum dwelling communities, consist of young men who have recently come to the capital from neighboring Bihar state to find employment. A few women and children live in the *basti*, but more commonly, domestic groups are made up of single men who live and work together. They all speak their own language dialect and maintain separate lives from other nearby slum dwellers who have arrived from other states of India.

Family Operations

The way a family operates can be a fascinating area of study. Family values, decision making, and family problems shed light on fundamental aspects of each individual's life. Honor and shame can be deeply ingrained values that determine normal interactions between family members and outsiders. To pursue an understanding of family operations, gather case histories of family interactions. Get a feel for how family members influence one another and use their relationships for leverage. Who owes what to whom? What are the typical

In some church-planting situations, whole families have decided to follow Christ together.

expectations of a grandfather, mother, brother, or uncle, etc.? What would the ideal family be like in this society? What is the worst thing that can be done in the family? What common mistakes do family members make? How much interaction with those outside the family do various members have?

Decision making in the family is one area to explore. In some church-planting situations, whole families have decided to follow Christ together. When this has happened successfully, it has often been because the gospel has been presented in ways that align with patterns of decision making that already exist within the family unit. Therefore, understanding decision making within families might help in forming relevant evangelistic strategies. For example, a group of new missionaries saw that in the people group they were working among, the father of every family held power over the decisions of everyone else. These missionaries decided to build strong, trusting relationships primarily with fathers rather than with sons of their own age. This effort proved strategic, because the fathers' interest in the gospel began to influence everyone in their families.

Marriage decisions within the family can be quite significant.

In another case, a young missionary team leader realized that grandfathers held such sway over everyone else that his own youth might prevent the acceptance of the gospel among a particular people group. He decided to make a concerted effort to recruit older workers to join his church-planting team.

To understand decision making, learn what decisions are considered routine and who makes them. What kinds of decisions are special? How are they made? Who is responsible for which activities and which decisions? In the family, who wields authority in which areas and how?

Marriage decisions within the family can be quite significant and affect church-planting strategy in two ways. First, decisions about who is acceptable for marriage and who is not can boldly illustrate the operation of people group dynamics. If a *Thai-teh* (or "true" Thai) man would be disowned by his family and community for marrying a Chinese woman, perhaps barriers of understanding and acceptance that exist between these two groups indicate a need for separate church-planting efforts. Second, values and decisions regarding marriage may dramatically influence the story of a young Christian convert. What might be done if a young believer has been betrothed since birth to the Buddhist priest's daughter? How might a young Turkish man who has chosen to follow Christ find a believing young woman to marry?

When you pursue information about marriage decisions, look for the following things. Ideally, how are marriage partners chosen? What marriages or practices are not desired or tolerated? Who marries whom? How is it done? What is the process? What is prohibited? Gather everything possible about how marriages are arranged, approved, and consummated. How and why might marriages be ended?

Common family problems and pressures can also reveal ways that families typically operate. These problems help you discern the troubles that concern people deeply. Felt needs in family relationships can be touched with hope and power by the message of Christ. Try to inventory typical family problems. Get a feel for what brings anguish to the family and its different members. Watch for impression management, when people only tell you what they want you to think, not what is actually true. Try to collect real life stories from your cultural helper's point of view.

Pursue *their* perspective on family problems, not your projection of what is wrong with relationships. For example, most Christians are appalled by the Islamic practice of polygamy. In many cases, we have discovered bitter jealousies and deep pain among the wives of one husband. However, we were surprised by a cultural helper who was happy as a second wife. She truly considered herself privileged to be married to a prominent leader whom she loved dearly. Her relationship with the first wife was like that of two loving sisters. Though difficult to accept, we could not make a blanket generalization regarding the problems of Muslim families with more than one wife.

Associations and Institutions

Whenever people organize themselves for a common interest or purpose, the resulting social entity is called an association. If such associations evolve over time they may formalize as organizations or institutions. Clubs, secret societies, even informal gatherings can be considered associations. Associations and institutions are at the heart of social organization. Most important, a church is also an association.

We want to study associations and institutions because they show us locally acceptable forms and structures for the embryonic church. The Church is a unique association, but it is still clothed in human, social realities. To the degree that existing gatherings of people reflect acceptable forms of relating as a group or community, we can predict forms that a church might take in the future and the

What cultural aspects of gathering together as a group will be best to encourage in the new church?

context in which a believing fellowship would be formed. What cultural aspects of gathering together as a group will be best to encourage in the new church?

Research objectives for associations and institutions include:

- *Describing social gathering patterns for everyone: men, women, and children*

- *Learning what makes a "good" or desirable gathering*

- *Describing how religious groups become formalized, legalized, or tolerated*

- *Learning about institutions that might serve or oppose the gospel*

- *Participating in an important community gathering with your cultural helper*

White Beards

As is true in any culture, the church among Kazakh people needs godly men in leadership roles. In traditional Kazakh society, which is patriarchal, the respected leaders are older men, called aksakal, *translated "white beard." They are valued and honored for their wisdom.*

Today Kazakhs still look to older men for leadership, especially those who are honest and trustworthy. In many ways, older men will best influence the people of their communities in the spread of the gospel. One Kazakh believer said, "One of our greatest needs is for men. We need men to teach and preach in the villages."

Currently only a handful of Kazakh men have submitted their lives to the lordship of Jesus Christ. Christian workers struggle with how to reach the men and how best to provide leadership for groups of women converts.

An example of the significance of associations and institutions to church planting comes from Indonesia. In each *kampung* (traditional neighborhood) you will usually find a *pos*. The *pos* is a small, elevated shack where young men from the village sit and talk with each other. *Kampung*-based friendships for men are built at the *pos* where games of *batu* (dominoes) and *chatur* (chess) are played. In the eyes of a church planter, the *pos* could be a significant social meeting place in the *kampung* – a place where the gospel might be shared in a way that would fit naturally with the social structure of the people.

Leadership

Identifying and training godly leaders who can become pastors and elders is a leading problem in frontier mission situations. Getting the right people to lead in the best and most biblical way is a great challenge anywhere. You can glean insight into these problems by identifying who good leaders are and how they lead. Some missionaries use a model of leadership that comes from their culture instead of the culture of the people. A careful study of what a society hopes for and expects from its own leaders helps missionaries avoid promoting unfamiliar leadership styles in new churches.

To begin studying leadership, gather profiles of leaders who are esteemed on a community level. Who is not esteemed? Why? Discover different functions and types of leaders. Describe how disputes are settled, how decisions are made, and how plans for the future are set. Describe how community leaders are recognized or chosen.

A situation in Thailand illustrates the usefulness of studying leadership. The church that thrives in Bangkok is primarily of Chinese descent. Among the Chinese, family and clan associations are common and their leadership style is hierarchical. A Chinese pastor is seen as the head. Responsibility in the church is delegated from higher to lower ranks. But the Thai leadership style is distinct. Thais look for a leader who is self-effacing and non-directive. A Thai will not readily put himself forward for leadership, neither will he hand down decisions to those beneath him. This reserve is not disinterest or lack of motivation, but polite behavior.

In addition, *barami* is a central concept in Thai leadership patterns. Devotion, support, and submission are given to one man who is recognized as the leader. The greater his following, the greater his *barami* grows. While such a leader will be non-directive, his words and opinions will be taken seriously.

The differences in Chinese and Thai leadership styles have implications for church planting in Bangkok. In general, Thai people are not drawn to Chinese-style churches. How will churches for the Thai look different from Chinese churches in terms of leadership? What culturally valued traits might a missionary look for and encourage when selecting and training true Thai leaders? These questions can be more fully answered by studying leadership as a facet of social structure.

The Ebb and Flow: Social Dynamics

To understand social dynamics is to unveil the ways that communities are being pushed or shaped by certain forces. People cannot be completely cloistered away from the impact their governments, their economy, their education, or various other factors are having on them. We need to see what impact social dynamics have had in the past and are having in the present. These dynamics may be preparing peoples for the gospel or hindering them from receiving it. Cities are particularly dynamic. Exploring social dynamics is like taking a step back to view the overall picture into which people groups fit.

Many factors tend to shape societies and cause cultural change. Eight common ones we have encountered are: urbanization and migration, modernization, religion, education, government policy and economics, communication, history, and demographics. A study of social dynamics can expand and inform your approach to church planting in at least two ways. First, you will learn about and be able to anticipate the needs, fears, and hopes of the people. Your understanding may lead you to choose evangelistic approaches that are relevant and appropriate for your target audience. Finally, you can begin to anticipate the environment in which you will live and minister. A long-range perspective will be needed.

Urbanization and Migration

Urbanization is the movement of people to the city, and it can also refer to the dynamic among migrants of adopting an urban lifestyle. Targeting a migrant community in the city may be strategic if people there are more receptive to the gospel than those who live in the homeland. Communication ties between the city

In Turkey, Kurdish migrants can be grouped according to various stages of migration.

and village may serve to spread the gospel from city dwellers to friends and relatives elsewhere. On the other hand, a migrant community in the city may be so transient that effective, long-term ministry among that people group would better occur in the homeland. In either case, a study of urbanization can shed light on such targeting issues.

Key questions to pursue are "Who is moving to the city, from where and why?" and "What happens when they arrive and adapt to their new setting?" Migration itself is a complex phenomenon. For example, in Turkey, Kurdish migrants in large cities can be grouped according to various stages of migration. Kurds who have lived in the city for twenty or more years are quite different from those who have recently arrived and settled, literally overnight, by building *gecekondus*. *Gecekondus* are shanties of wood, cardboard, and metal scraps that are built under cover of night on someone's unguarded property. In other cases, as in Indonesia, Muslim men regularly set out on a *rantau* – a journey to the city to find success. These young men can be found at universities, or coming and going in the city's areas of business and trade. They may live with relatives or stay in local *losmens*, which are similar to youth hostels.

Urbanization is a complex, often erratic, and yet constant process. To understand urbanization you can describe the different patterns of migration, locate and investigate different migrant communities, and look for the persistence or mutation of rural social patterns. Describe urban-rural communication channels. Take an inventory of motivations, needs, and tensions related to urbanization.

Migration Patterns

A move to the city often begins with a time of exploration and visiting. Soon one or two of the strongest or younger family members are sent to the city – or they may set out on their own. Once they arrive in the city, they may join other friends or family already living there. A bewildering time of instability can last for a week or perhaps as long as a decade. Establishment in the city and assimilation of an urban lifestyle can be slowed or extended by visits back to the home region for special occasions or agricultural seasons. For example, a community of young Kurdish men live and work in Damascus during the winter months, but they return to their villages for spring planting and fall harvesting each year. Most of these men marry Kurdish women from their village or region of origin rather than marrying city girls. Seek to understand the typical cycle or process of urbanization. Does temporary migration occur? Do people stay in the city for a few months or for years?

Locate Migrant Communities

Sometimes whole villages are re-established in the midst of cities. For example, Bombay has slum areas where the majority of the residents are Bihari Muslims. They continue to use their own language, wear their native dress, and celebrate holidays with their own regional flair. Such symbols of the culture or village of origin help urban migrant groups maintain boundaries between themselves and the rest of the city.

Small pockets of different migrant groups may exist throughout the city or be concentrated in particular parts of town. To locate migrant communities you can explore neighborhoods one by one or investigate outlying areas dubbed the "urban sprawl." Native residents often know about migrants and where they are located. Many will express derogatory opinions about such newcomers. Though you may learn about migrant communities second-hand by talking with a particular cultural helper, it is best to visit migrant communities yourself.

For example, in New Delhi, Muslims who lived in the Old City told us that migrant communities of other Muslims could be found across the river. However, they said they would never go there (and neither should we if we hoped to remain safe from murderers and hoodlums). A journey across the river revealed a huge migrant population – and no lurking criminals. Neighborhoods with schools and mosques had been established, though the community lacked amenities such as running water and electricity. New cultural helpers, of course, described their community better than prejudiced outsiders could.

Change in the Urban Setting

A move to the city can set in motion irreversible changes within families that will eventually affect the lifestyle and values of an entire community. Generation gaps

A bewildering time of instability can last for a week or as long as a decade.

may widen, separating children in significant ways from their parents, or portions of families from the roots they once had in the village. For instance, children educated in a trade language in the city may lose their ability or change their attitudes about speaking their mother tongue outside of the home. In Uzbekistan, most Uzbeks in the capital city speak Russian as well as Uzbek. Uzbeks from the city are no longer considered to be pure representatives of traditional Uzbek culture because they have adopted Russian language and lifestyles and have lost the practice of time-honored customs.

On the other hand, rural values can be embraced even more vigorously in the city as a reactionary stance against assimilation. Rural peoples in urban settings may cling to their regional identity even more tightly than before.

Urban life can significantly shape a generation's world view. Exposure to new ideas, moral options, and the influence of pop culture in the city all contribute to the adoption of some cosmopolitan characteristics. Old, rural ways are often left behind. Explore the changes that people describe and how they feel about them. What changes are valued and which are shunned or despised? What values, beliefs, and social patterns persist and which ones are changing?

A move to the city can set in motion irreversible changes within families that will affect the lifestyles and values of an entire community.

Communication Channels

Another aspect of urbanization pertains to relationships and communication channels between city migrants and their friends and family back home. The

character of these communication channels might indicate whether or not the gospel would spread from new believers in the city back to their region of origin. Researchers in Indonesia considered whether or not a ministry focused on reaching young men who were in the city because of *rantau* might be effective. These young men might be more open to the gospel, and their influence back at home after "finding success" in the city seemed to be very high. It also seemed more feasible for Christian workers to be based in urban areas rather than in rural villages. How would village dwellers hear the gospel? The practice of *rantau* could be a key.

In another case, we discovered that church-planting efforts conducted in Russian among Russified Kazakhs in the city would not be respected or accepted if reproduced in rural areas or villages. Few Russified Kazakhs maintained relationships with traditional Kazakhs through which the gospel might spread. A more traditional approach

conducted in Kazakh would be needed in addition to effective Russian language ministries in the cities.

Most migrants to the city can describe a host of physical and emotional needs.

Motivations

Seek to understand why families and individuals take the plunge into the city. Find out what motivates them. Why is the grass "greener," or is it? Are they happy or do most return to the countryside as soon as they can? If migrants dream of returning, do they actually ever leave the city? Are migrations voluntary? Sometimes economic or political hardships force many people to cities against their will. For example, many Palestinians in Damascus originally settled in refugee camps when their land was annexed by Israel. They had little choice in the matter. Now, these camps have been transformed into functional Palestinian neighborhoods which have existed for more than twenty years.

If migration is a factor in your situation, trace its process and the typical patterns of migration. How do relationships between people in the city and those back home change? Try to collect stories from migrants themselves.

Felt Needs

Most migrants to the city can describe a host of physical and emotional needs. Their whole lives may be in turmoil due to the pressures of urbanization. In some cases, the need for adequate and accessible health care can be staggering. Others need help in learning a new language and in finding quality education for their children. Christian workers may gain access to isolated people groups through development work or advocacy among migrants. Many migrants experience deep loneliness in the city; they feel isolated from others who are well-established in the city. Befriending people like this can lead to new opportunities to share Christ and to minister to felt needs.

"Things are changing so fast in our city."

Modernization

Modernization is closely related to urbanization because it may be one of the changes that occurs with a move to the city. Understand how people's lifestyles are changing because of new technology or new ideologies. How does a family's lifestyle today compare to what it was like ten years ago? Visualize where people in the city have come from in the recent past and the impact modernization might have in years to come. For example, a cultural helper in Malaysia spoke about modernization in this way, "Things are changing so fast in our city. Now, young people are not as concerned about family, and they pursue careers instead. *Kampungs* [traditional Malay neighborhoods] are less and less common, people live in *tamans* [modern neighborhoods] now. Houses are being built on the ground, not up on stilts like we used to build them." Responses like this may help you understand who to target, their felt needs, and the environment in which you will be ministering.

Religion

While religion may also be a topic of interest in regard to social stratification (i.e., Does religion contribute to people group distinctions?), it is also a topic to be considered as a forceful social dynamic. Particularly, you should explore people's overall attitudes toward religion and how their attitudes are being shaped by religious ideas.

In some urban settings, the overall tone of religious life leans toward the secular. People may not have time for strict religious requirements and may be more concerned with "things of the world" than with spiritual life. Secularization may be practically complete, as among some modern Turks who are Muslim in name only and who have been educated in European universities.

In other cases, superstition and folk practice characterize the tone of religious life. In Kazakhstan, traditional superstitions and folk practices are on the rise. It would not be uncommon for a Kazakh professional to state that he is a Muslim who no longer believes in God. Later, you might find that he offers a sacrifice each Thursday to appease the dead spirit of his grandfather.

Other people groups or cultures experience trends toward fundamental, orthodox beliefs. For example, in parts of Indonesia fundamentalists launched campaigns to educate the people in orthodox Islam. They mocked folk practices as carryovers from pagan religions. Sometimes such efforts fall on deaf ears, but in this case many people accepted this movement toward fundamental Islamic belief and practice.

Trends toward secularization, superstition, or fundamentalization can reveal valuable information for Christian workers. First, you gain specific information about the religious beliefs and ideas of a culture. To whom do people turn in times of crisis? What do they think about man's origin and destiny? What do they think will provide a full and meaningful life? What religious beliefs or moral system do they actually try to live by?

Second, you may begin to sense particular spiritual strongholds or influences that need to be overcome so that people can hear and respond to the gospel. Prayer efforts can be mobilized to stand against a particular cloud of darkness that blinds the people to the grace and beauty of Christ.

Effective approaches for Christian evangelism might also be revealed as you study the social dynamic of religion. For example, it became apparent after spending time with Turkmen that their pervasive concern about evil spirits would need to be factored into any church-planting effort among them. You might assume that 70 years of Communist ideology would require missionaries to use

Gain specific information about the religious beliefs and ideas of a culture.

apologetic tactics, or that Turkmen's Islamic heritage would require workers to have knowledge of Islam and the *Qur'an*. But in reality, traditional Turkmen are more concerned about the unseen spiritual world than they are about maintaining atheism or upholding the five pillars of Islam.

Education

Education in a community plays a role in shaping the people who live there. You need at least a cursory understanding of how education works, its availability, and its influence on the lives of people. Sometimes differences in education levels or forms affect people group distinctions. For example, Kazakhs who attend Russian schools are quite different from those who attend Kazakh schools. Education is also a general social dynamic and its overall influence should be noted. Consider education in the whole scheme of things. How is it shaping a particular community? What are people's concerns and hopes in regard to education? Is education valued, or obtainable, and for what reasons?

Government Policy and Economics

Government policy and economics obviously affect people and their daily lives. Sometimes tensions run high. Understanding the root of such tensions will help you gain perspective on the whole picture of a country and its people. How might political and economic realities affect a people group over the next ten years? What kind of situation will Christian workers find?

Education: The KEY?

Much like a typical middle class father in the United States, Abdul wants his children to be offered greater opportunities than he's had. "I want to be defeated by my son." The road to such opportunity, in Abdul's mind, is education. "Education is the only way through which we can raise ourselves up."

Those in the Urdu-speaking Middle Class of North India can afford private education or will do whatever is necessary to get it. Within this class the mentality is, "If you are born you have to study. If you don't, you are nothing."

Government policy and economics affect people and their daily lives.

The significance of government agendas and the economic situation of a country can be illustrated through examples of research done in Malaysia and the former Soviet Union. In Malaysia, a government policy grants Malay people special status over citizens of Chinese and Indian descent. This *bumiputra* status of the Malays gives them advantages when it comes to government employment and higher education. This government policy touches the lives of every person living in Malaysia. The ramifications are so widespread that one's approach to church-planting issues and options would be hindered considerably without understanding the policy, and how it is perceived, used, and circumvented by the people.

In many parts of the former Soviet Union an understanding of economics (both past, present, and hoped for) is needed to relate with the people. Why are there bread lines? What has it meant for your cultural helper and his family to face inflation rates of 1000 percent per year for each year since communism fell? What is the meaning of rubles and U.S. dollars in an economy in complete disarray? Understanding the economy can help answer some questions related to Christian ministry.

Communication

Another social dynamic that moves and shapes people groups is communication trends. Subtleties of communication cannot be fully understood without fluent use of the native language, but some aspects of communication can be still be noted. For instance, what are people reading or listening to? Where are they traveling and what kinds of questions are they asking other people?

Among the Kazakhs, legends, poetry, and music are significant forms of communication.

In terms of the media and its influence, consider the kinds of media people prefer. For example, look at the availability and use of books, magazines, newspapers, leaflets, comics, radio, VCR, television, drama, music, demonstrations – the list could go on. Which forms are widely used, and which are virtually useless?

Styles of verbal communication can also be observed. What types of communication are used? Do people prefer nonfiction, narrative, poetry, myth, proverbs, or debates? What ways of communicating are used? Do people prefer frankness or subtlety?

For example, among the Kazakhs, legends, poetry and music are significant forms of communication. Abaya Konambaev, a famous Kazakh author and poet once said, "Kazakh people come to life with music and leave life with music."

When a baby is born, when someone dies, and when a man and woman are married – the Kazakhs sing. In addition, Kazakhs today continue the ancient tradition of competing with each other in poetry-singing contests called *aytis*. During an *aytis*, musicians improvise poetry that is sung to melodies. The melodies are also improvised. The objective of the *atyis* is for one musician to outwit the other. First one musician sings and then the other answers. Whoever is unable to answer cleverly loses. The content of the poetry-songs varies but often includes ideas about love, beauty, honor, social problems, and political ideas. Boasts of one's city or *zhuz* (tribe) are also common. By studying types and styles of communication, it became apparent that music, poetry, and legends would have great significance for evangelism and discipleship among Kazakhs. Kazakh believers are now writing their own worship music.

history

The present and future must be interpreted by the past. Therefore, the events of the past and their influence on a people group are extremely significant. history can be learned to some extent by reading textbooks. But the most interesting stories are usually told by elderly people. What do people consider to be the significant events of the last 30 years? of the last 500 years? How have they reacted to these events? Your cultural helper's thoughts, insights, memories, stories, and impressions regarding the past will expand and inform any cultural interpretations that you make.

Doing ethnographic research is like entering the timeline of a people. With broad strokes, the information you gather will paint a picture of where they have come from and where they are going. Your presence as learners, as prayer warriors, and as representatives of the kingdom of God will mark their story in some way – perhaps for eternity. In addition, you have the vantage point of knowing that God's hand has certainly been at work throughout history to prepare a particular people group to respond to his grace and salvation. History *is* his story! All that you learn about the past can be considered in light of this eternal perspective.

The most interesting stories are usually told by elderly people.

Demographic Information

In most urban areas, you can find demographic information about the country and perhaps even the city you are studying. Gather data from libraries and institutes (government and private) on language, ethnicity, age, gender, and occupation. Talk with sociologists, city officials, and other experts about statistics and projections for the future. Other Christian workers in the city may also know about resources. Ask particularly about information they consider significant and what insights they have used to shape their ministry. What information have they been unable to locate? Demographic information can be used to briefly describe the people's physical environment, and statistics can be used to describe the country or city as a whole. What are the local natural resources? What common products are made for home use or for sale?

Statistics are not always the most helpful in understanding the complexity of another culture. Sometimes figures published by the government or by other "official" groups are skewed by their own agenda, or are outdated quickly. But when figures can be added to the "soft data" you are learning from real people, statistical information can solidify or verify some conclusions that you are formulating. Demographic information can also raise your awareness of the big picture – of the macrocosm of a whole country or city. Information regarding natural resources, certain projections for the future, population and growth statistics, or current economic trends are usually available.

A Loving God?

Ahmed and his family live in a predominately Palestinian neighborhood in Damascus. his voice cracked with emotion as he related his family's story, "I was three years old when we fled Palestine, but my father decided to remain and fight. He was killed in the struggle that year and my mother had to find a way for us to survive in Damascus. Her constant anguish and today's daily news of the Palestinian conflict continue to remind me of my pain."

Ahmed finds it hard to believe in a God who would allow such suffering and injustice.

In one case, statistical information affected our understanding of people in Syria. Several government documents stated that over half of the population of Syria in 1990 was under the age of 15. This statistic grievously confirmed the stories we had gathered from many families. War in the Middle East has had a tremendous impact on previous and current generations. Most families have lost grandfathers, fathers, or older brothers in some military conflict. In addition, we saw the need for Christian ministry among children and youth since they represent half of the country's entire population.

The Hound of Heaven: Evangelization

Before you interpret cultural information to form effective strategies for church planting, you must explore one final area of interest. To evaluate the future of evangelization for a group, you must explore three aspects of their past exposure to Christianity. First, what has been their exposure, if any, to Christianity? Second, if there are believers already among a people group, what has been their story of conversion and growth in Christ? And third, how receptive do the people seem to be? These questions correspond to the research topics of history of evangelization, church growth, and receptivity.

In some instances, as in Thailand and parts of India, our teams needed to gather a great deal of information about people's past and present exposure to Christianity. Missionaries have had a witness in Thailand for more than 1200 years, and it is rumored that St. Thomas, the disciple who doubted Jesus' resurrection, was the first missionary to India. The church that thrives in Thailand is primarily of Chinese descent, and long-standing Christian movements exist among tribal groups and the Isaan of northeastern Thailand. But still, there are very few Christian converts among those who regard themselves as pure Thai people, the *Thai-teh*. In settings like Thailand, an understanding of the history of evangelization, of church growth, and receptivity is essential. Few urban situations will yield absolutely nothing about these topics.

A Glimmer of Hope

Each month a small group of evangelical pastors gather for prayer and encouragement. These visionary men are seeking God for the evangelization of their city. In the midst of a largely stagnant church, they are taking a stand, calling the church to reach out to the lost, to respond to the needs of the poor, and to make a difference in their city.

A word of exhortation needs to be added here. Any exploration of these topics must be done humbly, with the same learner's attitude that would mark interviews with any cultural helper. We have been tempted to pass judgment on what fellow believers have done to share the gospel. But investigating past and current ministry, learning the stories of Christian converts, and making statements about a people's receptivity to the gospel must be carried out with a servant's heart, for the sake of coming alongside others who hope to see the kingdom of God further established. In addition, the personal security and well-being of missionaries and Christian converts, and their own work among unreached people groups is more important than gathering information. Never, never jeopardize these brothers and sisters by your own curiosity and naivete. Your contact with converts may cause them to be unduly scrutinized by officials or by antagonistic family members. Ask permission and build trust before exploring. Pray. May your learning efforts only serve to build up and encourage the church of our Lord Jesus!

history of Evangelization

Key questions to explore the history of evangelization among a particular people group are: What styles and methods of evangelism have been tried? What has been the result? Collect stories of evangelistic outreaches, of church-planting

efforts, and of conversion among the people. Have different mission efforts had strengths or weaknesses that can inform future efforts? What external factors or cultural realities may have contributed to their success or failure? Are there current ministry trends? Why do they exist and what do they mean for effective church planting?

What styles and methods of evangelism have been tried? What has been the result?

At least three groups of people can help to answer these questions. They are long-term missionary workers, national leaders, and converts (if there are any) of the people group you are researching. In addition, short-term workers may also have valuable insights, though their opinions will be less proven by time and experience.

When you begin to plan a research project, include as many of these people as possible. Ask whether they would be willing or able to talk with you about their experiences. If not, don't pry. It may be most difficult to contact new converts in hostile situations. Before even attempting to do so, ask for the advice or permission of local missionaries before approaching a convert. Take time to build trust, and do not betray that trust. If you have the privilege of talking with missionaries, do not fall into the trap of taking sides and criticizing other missionaries. It is possible to honestly analyze and evaluate, without passing judgment. We always try to honor missionaries as our heroes. They are actually doing the work of the gospel. You must also respect churches of other ethnicities that are found among unreached peoples. They cannot be easily condemned for not reaching out to the lost around them. We may know little about the great persecution they have faced in the past, or what they would face if they were to act more boldly. Take time to understand the whole story from their perspective.

Church Growth

If fellowships of believers exist among your people group, learn their stories. How did churches form? What struggles and victories have they experienced? Are fellowships growing? If so, how and why?

The term "church growth" was coined by missiologist Dr. Donald MacGavran. In recent years, church-growth thinking has focused on the growth and decline of

Issues for New Believers

A number of issues and challenges face new Kazakh believers who are hungry to know more about Christ. Zhanna is one of those new believers.

"I am so happy because I've become a Christian. Though I accepted Jesus Christ last year, I was confused and afraid to tell people because of my nationality. Now I know that no matter what nationality you are, you may let Jesus into your life. But I realize that many Kazakhs will accuse me of betraying our people."

Zhanna's fear has become a reality. One Kazakh girl told Zhanna, "This is a time when we are renewing our Kazakh traditions and you are abandoning your traditions by becoming a Christian." Zhanna recalls, "After talking to this girl, I had some very difficult days. I began to think that maybe Christianity is just a story."

As these believers are searching for their identity, they need a church that will allow them to be fully Kazakh and fully Christian.

churches. Especially in America, the topic has become controversial. Some feel that studying church growth can increase the church's impact on society, while others feel that church growth techniques merely adopt worldly methods of marketing and advertising. Despite the recent controversy, studying church growth on the mission field is important to us in two areas: the ethnicity of churches and the indigeneity of churches.

After you have defined the different people groups in a city, look at churches that exist and see which people groups are represented in which churches. This will help you determine how accessible the gospel is to various people groups. Are churches ethnically homogenous or are they mixed? Who might be overlooked or unwelcome in current gatherings? Are groups of people so culturally distinct that they would not naturally attend any of the churches that exist in the city?

Related to, but distinct from the ethnicity of churches, is the indigeneity of churches. While ethnicity refers to the people group make-up of a particular church, indigeneity refers to the degree to which a church is patterned in ways that are appropriate to its culture. If a church is indigenous, that means it is "naturally" occurring and is relevant to the people of a particular culture.

Indigeneity is difficult to gauge without a complete understanding of evangelization and without living among the people for a long time. Yet if it is possible, try to understand indigenous or non-indigenous aspects of the church to form your own ideas about effective church planting. Observing forms of worship, language of worship and music, leadership structure, and style of communication may help you determine indigeneity. Another way to gauge indigeneity is to ask non-Christians about their perceptions of the church.

Receptivity

Receptivity to the gospel is a slippery notion in missions circles. How can you really know whether a particular people group is more open than another to seriously considering the change that is involved in following Christ? In reality, you can't know for sure.

What you say about receptivity is very important because people are influenced by it. Your work might help remove a stigma that certain people groups are impossible to reach for Christ. We have seen that saying, "This people is so receptive to the gospel!" often serves to motivate the church to begin new missionary efforts. Yet to say the opposite may turn many away from a work that so desperately needs to be done.

Receptivity should not be confused with congeniality to outsiders. Muslim fundamentalists may be congenial to those they hope to proselytize, but have no intention of following Jesus. (On the other hand, some are sincerely interested and have turned into excellent evangelists after following Jesus.) Some groups such as university professors and the educated elite enjoy entertaining and debating new ideas, but may not be interested in the gospel for themselves. Even in Bible times, the men of Athens in Acts 17 loved ideas, but not the Lord.

If people are not receptive to a Western version of Christianity or to the type of Christianity known in your own culture, this may not necessarily indicate an unwillingness to follow Christ in biblical obedience. If people have been unresponsive, they may not always be so. Perhaps they would be responsive to another approach or embodiment of the Christian message.

When characterizing a people group's receptivity, look carefully at the group as a whole and not just at individuals. You may find "receptive" individuals in a non-receptive group, or visa versa. Also, speak of degrees of receptivity instead of black or white terms like receptive or not receptive.

The most obvious indicator of receptivity is the number of converts from a particular people group. However, among unreached peoples, this indicator is not usually available. The following social variables may also help you subjectively discern receptivity among a particular people. These variables are *kairos*, crisis, status inconsistency, and alienation.

Kairos

Sometimes, through study and prayer, you will sense that God's time (*kairos* – Greek) has come for a certain people group to begin to follow him. Once, a Caleb Project research team in a South Asian city felt that God had prepared a people group in the city for a significant spiritual work. People within the group felt that their community was coming to a crisis point. Their spiritual leader was increasing his hold on the community even while a reform movement was gaining power. The team felt that major changes would come to the community in the near future that would increase their openness to the gospel.

In other cases, the question of receptivity to the gospel can be investigated by exploring indicators of flexibility, tension, need, and fear in various people groups. Clues about receptivity may be found by gathering stories of individuals or families who have recently responded to the gospel. Comparison of these factors can be made between various groups, perhaps indicating that one group, more than another, seems ready to receive the message of Christ.

Crisis

If a people group has experienced a crisis, they may ask why disaster has happened to them. Their bereavement can indicate an openness to the gospel message. For example, many peoples of the former Soviet Union are experiencing an ideological crisis, as well as a time of economic chaos. A spiritual vacuum exists, and many are showing signs of unprecedented receptivity. Sometimes crises or tragic events such as earthquakes, floods, and famine can soften people's hearts to spiritual realities.

Status Inconsistency

Status inconsistency exists whenever a group's position on one scale differs considerably from their logical status on a second scale. For example, individuals with high educational status could also be characterized by low economic or political status. This is unexpected since most highly educated people do well financially. We have found that people measure status in different ways. Some measure education and occupation, others look to levels of secularization or modernization, while still others measure status according to other factors. Where there is status inconsistency, people's hopes are shaken – their disappointment and confusion about what life is all about increases. Such a group may be more receptive than those who exhibit no disparity between status scales.

An example of status inconsistency can be seen in the situation of students and university professors in Ashgabat, Turkmenistan. Ashgabat is home to one university and twelve institutes of higher education. The quality of instruction is declining as teachers and good students leave to make higher wages working for private firms. Teaching was once prestigious and profitable. Today it is neither. Now many students who would have worked as English teachers are aiming for jobs as Russian-English or Turkmen-English translators for foreign firms. One professor described his situation: "We earn 600 *manat* per month. At one time that was $300 but because of inflation it is now $10. That is very little for life." Students and university professors are both experiencing status inconsistency.

Alienation

The term "alienation" is used to refer to groups who feel separated from and discontent with society. They are dissatisfied and feel alone in what appears to be a hopeless situation. To the extent that people within a group are feeling alienated, this factor can be a useful indicator of receptivity. Those who are alienated may be searching for meaning in life because they are unable to find fulfillment in their work or in their culture. They may give up their search for meaning in the material world and become receptive to the spiritual realm. New ideas, expressions of creativity, and a desire for deeper interpersonal relationships may give them hope for finding significance and purpose. When groups of people are at such a junction, they may receive the gospel more easily.

Kairos, crisis, status inconsistency, and alienation are only four of many variables that may indicate a people's receptivity. Other factors such as unrest, dissatisfaction, or even an anticipation of something new can contribute to your understanding of receptivity among people groups.

Table 7 Part III Summary			
Who Are the Peoples?	**What Are They Like?**		**How Can They Be Reached?**
Who's Who in the Zoo **Stratification**	*The Warp & Woof* **Social Structure**	*The Ebb & Flow* **Social Dynamics**	*The Hound of Heaven* **Evangelization**
Purpose: *Discern the people groups*	**Purpose:** *Consider how people relate to others*	**Purpose:** *Understand the social evolution of the people – their past, present, and future*	**Purpose:** *Discover what God has already done to establish his church among a people*

Possible Topics:
Class brackets
Ethnicity
Language and dialects
Neighborhoods
Occupations
Religious beliefs
Political parties
Caste or tribal groups
Region of origin
Degree of secularization
Degree of modernization
Stage of migration
Education
Status, Role, Prestige
	Possible Topics:
	Network relationships
	Family and kinship
	  • *Family trees*
	  • *Family styles*
	  • *Family operations*
	Associations and institutions
	Leadership
		Possible Topics:
		Urbanization and migration
		Modernization
		Religion
		Education
		Government policy and economics
		Communication
			Possible Topics:
			history of evangelization
			Church growth
			Receptivity

Skills Introduced: *Building taxonomies* *Describing groups* *Ascertaining boundaries*	**Skills Introduced:** *Drawing networks* *Network analysis*	**Skills Introduced:** *No new skills*	**Skills Introduced:** *No new skills*

Making the Areas of Interest Work for You

As you gather information regarding stratification, social structure, social dynamics, and evangelization, you must put this information to work for your situation. You are now able to meld cultural and social realities with your desire to see a movement toward Christ in a particular country, city, or people group. To conclude Part III, let's return to the foundational perspective of *envisioning*. Recall the envisioning diagram presented earlier.

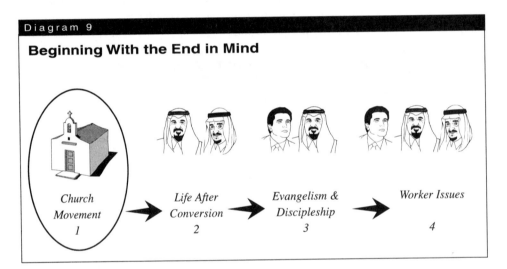

Diagram 9

Beginning With the End in Mind

Church Movement *1* → Life After Conversion *2* → Evangelism & Discipleship *3* → Worker Issues *4*

Remember that while pursuing these four areas of interest, you have been doing so "with the end in mind." Given what you *now* know about people groups in your city and what they are like, what might it be like for them to walk in obedience to Christ within their own culture? Such a sweeping question can be broken down into smaller parts: What might a church do in terms of her work and witness within the culture? What issues might new converts face in their life after conversion? Given the reality of such issues, how might effective evangelism and discipleship take place? And, in light of your vision to see people follow Christ, what must you do to prepare yourself for that work?

To help you assimilate the cultural information you have gathered using the four areas of interest outlined above, we have included a list of questions to consider. These questions suggest applications that can be made to your work as a church planter. Not all of these questions will apply, and other questions that are not included here may be more important for your situation. They are divided into four groups: questions pertaining to a church's work and witness, to life after conversion, to evangelism and discipleship, and to worker issues.

The Church's Work and Witness

- *How will believers in the church witness and add others to their fellowship?*

- *How will the church endure persecution and act to further world evangelization itself?*

- *How will the church relate to others such as churches of other ethnicities, daughter churches, and the Church worldwide?*

- *What social conditions should the church seek to transform? Needs might include medical care, education, employment, political reform, and poverty.*

Life After Conversion

- *How might new converts worship and celebrate?*

- *What are fitting cultural patterns for celebration?*

- *What other traditions might be adaptable or shed light on this issue?*

- *How will the community of believers build trusting relationships and share needs with each other? What will fellowship between believers look like in this culture?*

- *Will there be regular gatherings of believers? If so, how often? Where will they meet? For what purpose?*

- *Are there cultural symbols that should or shouldn't be present?*

- *What should the decor and arrangement of the meeting place look like?*

- *Will those who attend be from the same people group, or mixed? Who will come and who won't?*

- *What will be the legal status of the church – underground, registered with the government, or other?*

- *Will literature be used in the church? What is available? What needs to be developed? What forms should new resources take and what language or languages should be used?*

- *Are there other forms of communication that might be effective?*

- *How will finances be handled in the church? What are fitting cultural patterns for handling money?*

- *What will the church do about receiving and managing outside funds? How will they handle the collection, control, and allocation of local funds?*

- *How will the church recognize, select, and train leaders?*

- *What styles of leadership are culturally appropriate?*

- *What language is most appropriate for teaching and preaching the Bible?*

- *How will families function in godly ways?*

- *How will people receive pastoral care and be counseled in culturally appropriate ways?*

- *What role will signs, wonders, and spiritual gifts play in the life of the church?*

Evangelism and Discipleship

- *What evangelistic methods should be employed?*

- *What kind of decision to follow Christ do you want to work for: group, family, or multi-individual? Are there rites and rituals attached to decision making? Should you ask permission of an authority figure inside or outside the family or community before beginning evangelism or discipling a convert? How will adult decisions be different from those of children?*

- *At what points in society can you anticipate resistance to the gospel? How should you address barriers to a movement toward Christ among the people?*

- *How will you introduce repentance? What things, unique to the culture, might people repent from?*

- *What will you do about baptism? When should it take place? Where? By whom? As a witness to whom?*

- *How will you address issues that new converts face such as finding marriage partners, finding a job or education, dealing with family pressure, family life, and divorce?*

- *What things cause impure motives for conversion? Are there things you must consider when working through a person's reasons for conversion?*

- *How will you deal with converts who return to their old way of life? Why might people revert? Are some people more likely to revert than others?*

- *How will you counsel the convert who is experiencing persecution? Where does persecution come from? Are there ways it might be minimized? Would you suggest different kinds of counsel for different forms of persecution?*

- *Will westernization be an issue? Will people be drawn to the church because they view conversion as a way to become more "western?"*

- *Is unnecessary extraction from society taking place? How might extraction be minimized?*

- *How will you disciple and care for new converts?*

- *How will you facilitate culturally appropriate gatherings in the early stages of church planting? What settings will be safe or unsafe? How will you counsel new believers concerning their public witness? Should they remain "secret" believers or make their conversion public knowledge?*

Worker Issues

- *What people group should you target in this city?*

- *What kinds of people within a people group should you first seek relationships with?*

- *What will your identity be? Will some roles make you more or less effective in reaching a people group? What training will you need to fill that role?*

- *What types of people or networks might be strategic targets for evangelism within a people group?*

- *Where should you live in the city? What neighborhood? What type of housing?*

- *What security issues might you face in this country?*

- *What types of visas can you get? For how long? How does it work?*

- *What types of jobs are available for foreigners in this city?*

- *What language should you learn? How should you learn it? What are the possibilities?*

- *How will you relate to other missionaries to plan and work toward a culturally relevant church-planting movement?*

- *Who appears to be most accepted by the people? Who might reach them effectively? North Americans? Latin Americans? Koreans, etc.?*

- *Can you identify spiritual strongholds among a people group? How will prayer be mobilized for your work?*

Conclusion

The four areas of interest described here – stratification studies, social structure, social dynamics, and evangelization – form our particular approach to researching people groups in urban settings. The information must be applied to be of use. The list of church-planting questions has been included to help you meld people group information with real life issues in pioneer situations. Our desire is that you learn more about your city or target people group. Use and expand these four areas of interest in order to begin and complete your own investigations. The questions and examples we have provided are meant to stimulate your thinking about culture and to illustrate the fact that learning can lead to helpful insights regarding church planting.

Part IV:
Working It Out As A Team

We recognize that some readers will want to do ethnographic research as a team. This final section presents a case study based on the Caleb Project Research Expedition to Bangkok, Thailand in 1988. Rather than discussing aspects of team work that are common to all short-term mission trips, the following case study outlines unique elements of working out research as a team. Many of the ethnographic skills and each of the four areas of interest can be observed as they were put into action by our team in Bangkok. If you lack general information about developing a short-term missions experience, we recommend the annual handbook for short-term opportunities, *Into All the World* by Berry Publishing Services, Inc. and *Stepping Out: A Guide to Short-Term Missions* by YWAM publishing.

Finally, we will discuss in detail four areas that are particularly important for fielding successful research teams. These areas are team leadership, practice research, team debrief, and mobilization tools.

Caleb Project Research Expedition

Bangkok, Thailand, 1988

The Bangkok Research Expedition rose from a need for research that missionaries from Thailand expressed to us through a series of conversations. These missionaries indicated that most Christian work in Bangkok was being conducted among the ethnic Chinese rather than among the Thai people themselves. They were concerned that the gospel reach the Thai people as well.

A research design began to take shape. We determined to discover which people groups live in Bangkok and whether some groups were less reached than others. If the Thai people, or others, were being overlooked, why might that be so?

Prior to going to Bangkok, the team research coordinator (see page 149) invested a great deal of time networking with missionaries, national workers, and mission agencies working in Thailand. He interviewed nationals who came through our area and telephoned people in mission agencies whom we knew had worked, or were currently working, in Bangkok. He also gathered as much information as possible about Bangkok and its peoples. He ransacked local university research libraries and collected a number of resource and reference materials.

Team Training

Once team members were recruited and before they arrived for training, they raised the financial and prayer support they would need. They also began low-intensity study at their homes to prepare for their expedition. This period of pre-field training began in early October 1987 and lasted for thirteen weeks. By the time team members gathered at the Caleb Project office, they had read *The Ethnographic Interview* by James P. Spradley, major portions of *Stepping Out,* and some basic information about Bangkok and Thailand. The team leader had also read *Siamese Gold: A history of Church Growth in Thailand* by Alex G. Smith, along with other in-depth material about Thailand, modern sociology, and anthropology. Team members also read *Focus! The Power of People Group Thinking* by John D. Robb before they arrived.

Then the Bangkok team spent five weeks receiving classroom training and practical research experience. Team training focused on four key areas:

- *Foundations:* Material from *Part I: Building a Foundation* was presented.

- *Team Building:* Because we value team life and individual growth, this portion of team training emphasized spiritual

One of five weeks of training is given to building teamworking skills. These team members used a tinkertoy exercise to evaluate their ability to communicate and cooperate.

Table 8 Overview of Team Training Schedule

	Introduction to Caleb Project	Foundations				Prayerwalking
Day off	Team Building					Day off
	Research Skills				Country Specific Briefing	Day off
International Student Practicum	Field Practice: Cross-cultural Immersion					Day off
	Mobilization				Depart for Overseas	

Includes debrief of field practice, mobilization training, and last minute packing.

formation, cross-cultural living and coping skills, and effective team communication.

- **Research Skills and Field Practice:** Material from *Part II: Getting Ready* trained team members in ethnographic skills. *Part III: Going to Work* built the team's ability to pursue a specific research agenda. This portion of training also included practical research experience (see page 153) as well as country specific briefing. During country briefing, team members met some Thai nationals and had the opportunity to interview a Thai Christian convert.

- **Mobilization:** We do research primarily as a means to mobilize Christians to complete world evangelization. This part of training helped the team set goals for what they would do with their research and make plans for achieving those goals.

On the Field

After five weeks of training the team traveled together to Bangkok. The team was made up of fourteen people: two married couples, four single men, and six single women. Among them, one single man served as the team leader, providing pastoral care and overseeing the logistics of living and working overseas. Another young man served as the team's research coordinator. He provided oversight for all the research activities. Other special roles included a team photographer, treasurer, and another person who helped his teammates use computers and printers.

In Bangkok, the entire Caleb Project team stayed at a local guest house. Living together allowed the team to eat breakfast, pray, and worship together at the beginning of each day. In this setting they enjoyed mutual spiritual and emotional support. As one team member commented, "Unless you happen to be an extreme extrovert, it takes a lot of physical and emotional energy to keep going out day after day to initiate conversations and relationships!" Team members found that times of fellowship with one another and with God were vital for personal health as well as for encouragement in the task.

Research Stage 1: Exploration

The team's research included all four areas of interest – stratification, social structure, social dynamics, and evangelization – but began with an initial phase of broad exploration. The research coordinator took a map of the city and assigned various teamlets specific neighborhoods to visit. Their purpose was to explore an assigned area of the city, to discover what kinds of people lived there, and to see if they could locate English speakers in their section of the city. They wanted to

Bangkok team members initiated relationships wherever they could locate English-speaking nationals.

Table 9 In-Country Weekly Schedule						
Research	Research Reading filenotes	Strategy Meeting	Research	Research	Day off	Prayer-walking Mobilization Tools

establish relationships and build a sizeable pool of cultural helpers. Because they wanted a broad exposure to the city and its peoples, team members went back to the same cultural helpers no more than once or twice.

In addition to their initial explorations, team members attended a short series of Thai language classes. They learned enough language to get around the city comfortably. Bangkok team members initiated relationships on the street, in restaurants, in stores, and wherever they could locate English-speaking nationals. They also took time with their Thai friends to share about themselves. If their friends were interested, they showed pictures from home and practiced speaking English with cultural helpers. Many opportunities for participant observation opened up. A Thai friend invited the team to be honored guests at a wedding. Some teamlets were also invited to a museum while others visited their cultural helper's relatives in a nearby community.

At the end of each day, teamlets expanded their field notes into filenotes. They followed the standard format for writing filenotes described in Part II. Teamlet partners checked each other's notes after they were typed into the computers, made corrections and suggestions for greater clarity, and then printed a final copy of what they had written within 24 hours of an interview.

A Weekly Routine

During the team's first few weeks of exploration, a routine was established. Each week consisted of three and a half days of interviewing, a half day of reading filenotes, a day for strategy meetings, a day for prayerwalking and creating mobilization tools, and a day for rest and relaxation. (See Table 9 above.)

Strategy Meetings

With seven teamlets interviewing and recording fieldnotes, more than 100 pages of typed notes accumulated by the end of a week. A strategy meeting was needed. To "come up to speed" on each other's findings, all team members read everyone else's notes the day before the strategy meeting. Before they began reading, the research coordinator often assigned each team member a specific topic or angle to be especially aware of while reading. The idea was to have everyone familiar with all the data, yet prepared to interpret it from different perspectives.

The strategy meeting was held from 8:00 A.M. until around 5:00 P.M. After reviewing research goals from the previous week, team members discussed what their findings meant. Team members found that their data confirmed or conflicted with others' findings. Based on the strategy meeting discussion, decisions about what to study in the coming week were made.

Prayer Walks

Another part of the team's weekly routine was prayerwalking. Team members went out two by two to walk through and pray over specific areas of the city. The Bangkok team wanted to prayerwalk through the entire city. They kept a map on a wall at the guest house and colored in the areas where teamlets prayerwalked each week. This way they kept track of their prayer goal.

Throughout their experience, prayerwalking reminded team members of their ultimate purpose for doing research. As one expedition member commented,

> *Suddenly, as you are praying scripture for the people, you find your faith is built for what God can do. Prayerwalks give you a vision for what could happen. The significance of having a church established ... and what it will mean to the people, becomes a reality to you in a way that simply gathering more information can never do. More information can lead you to despair if you don't have anything to hang it on, something to build faith and hope.*

Another team member said,

> *As you pray about the facts and information that you know, you find that God gives you impressions of what the church could or will look like. The facts and information become translated into something imaginable through prayer.*

While prayerwalking, the Bangkok team saw the materialism of the city's Chinese population. They recognized the "godshelves" found in Chinese businesses and the Thai spirit houses in other shops. They often sensed spiritual oppression around Buddhist temples and felt that hedonism, alcoholism, and prostitution dominated the city in a spiritual way. These impressions factored into their overall understanding of Bangkok and the people living there.

Research Stage 2: Stratification Studies

About the beginning of the third week on the field, the Bangkok team shifted from exploration to focus on stratification studies. While teamlets continued to seek new cultural helpers throughout their visit, after the first couple of weeks they focused more energy on a few relationships.

Teamlets were assigned specific topics to study during the following week. With fourteen people and seven teamlets, the team studied at least three different stratification topics each week. Each topic was studied separately by two teamlets. Sometimes the teamlets required only a week to arrive at a strong consensus concerning a topic. At other times, they needed two or three weeks to complete their inquiries.

From their explorations, the team thought Bangkok residents would most likely view ethnicity, language, neighborhood, region of origin, and class as their primary differentiating characteristics. These stratification topics were assigned to various teamlets. Over the course of a few week's research, the team found that region of origin, ethnicity, and education/occupation (or class) were the primary ideas that residents actually used to distinguish themselves from one another. Each of these topics, however, received different emphases depending on the segment of the society.

The team then set out to analyze their filenotes to delineate Bangkok's people. What people groups could actually be found in Bangkok? Using the definition of a people group, the team made hypotheses about people groups in the city. Where would church-planting movements encounter barriers of understanding or acceptance if efforts were begun in various subsegments of Bangkok's broader society?

About the seventh week on the field, the team came to a consensus (though they felt they could do more research to test their people group hypotheses) that there are four major people groups in Bangkok: ethnic Chinese, ethnic Thai called the "*Thai-teh*," Chinese-Thai called the "*Thai-jin*," and *Isaan*, a tribal group from northeastern Thailand. The team was now ready to press on to new stages of research.

Research Stage 3: Going Deeper

While doing stratification studies, the team was exposed to most topics we have described related to social structure and social dynamics. Now the team shifted their focus from stratification to go deeper in their understanding of Bangkok's people groups. What were the Chinese, *Thai-teh*, *Thai-jin*, and *Isaan* like?

Many *Thai-teh* people in Bangkok migrated to the city from Central Thailand. The Isaan, however, came to the city from their villages in the Northeast. The team decided to spend a week surveying these areas of the country. The purpose

The team also began to ask questions about evangelization.

of their travel was to get a feel for the broader context of which Bangkok was a part. The team wanted to see, firsthand, the regions where people were coming from. They wanted to know what the people were like in their homeland.

The team split up into three groups and traveled to different regions of Thailand. In Central Thailand, one group observed and asked questions about a church planting effort called the "Thai Ezra" movement. The Thai Ezra model was proving to be successful among the *Thai-teh* people of Central Thailand. Missionaries were planting churches that fit the popular culture, and a modern Thai context. At the end of the week, the entire team regrouped in Udon Thani, a city in the Northeast. There they visited a missionary named Jim Gustafson. They wanted to observe his "contextualized development" approach to church planting among the *Isaan*. This approach, rather than fitting modern culture, was more traditional in character.

The team began their travels with a little information about the people groups in Bangkok. They ended their travels having built on their earlier understanding. The team came home seeing the *Thai-teh* and the *Isaan* more clearly and understanding them in deeper ways. They developed greater empathy for the *Isaan* who were living amidst the roar of Bangkok's traffic. The *Isaan* came from places where the fastest and noisiest form of transportation was a water buffalo!

They also understood more of the heart of *Thai-teh* culture after traveling outside the city. Distinctives that seemed blurred in Bangkok by intermarriage between some Chinese and Thai people became more evident than before. *Thai-jin* are much less common outside of Bangkok. Perhaps a better way to understand Bangkok society would be to see a spectrum of Chinese and Thai identity and allegiance. Extended families at the extremes of the Chinese-Thai spectrum would be either very Thai or firmly Chinese. The *Thai-jin* fall between the two extremes. The Chinese and Thai people have very different values and customs for relationships with family, for gathering together, and for leadership.

Research Stage 4: Evangelization

During their travels, the team also began to ask questions about evangelization. They talked with Christian workers in both Central and Northeastern Thailand and became familiar with gospel work being done there. They began to see how these effective ministry models might be used to reach people groups in Bangkok.

After returning to Bangkok, the team continued to focus on evangelization. A sizeable Christian presence exists there, so many questions could be asked. A particular question the team pursued was, "Are Bangkok's people groups equally represented in the churches?" This was one question that had sparked our interest in researching Bangkok in the first place.

To answer this question, team members visited churches, one teamlet per church, seven churches each Sunday morning. After the service they talked with church leaders and asked about the congregations' histories and about their current ethnic composition. In addition, team members interviewed some of Bangkok's more prominent Christian leaders, both national and missionary.

When team members talked with pastors, most said that some *Thai-teh* and *Isaan* members attended their congregations. When a pastor made such a comment, team members asked him to identify these people so they could interview them directly. When team members asked these individuals about their ethnic identity, almost every one identified himself or herself as Chinese or *Thai-jin*. In several instances, church leaders identified themselves and their churches as being Thai. However, it became clear that though they spoke the Thai language, culturally they were Chinese.

By the time the expedition was over, team members had visited nearly thirty churches in Bangkok. It turned out that, as the team had been told back in the United States, very few *Isaan* and even fewer *Thai-teh* populated the churches of Bangkok. No matter what language they spoke, almost all pastors were Chinese or *Thai-jin* and the members of their churches were Chinese or *Thai-jin* as well.

Research Stage 5: Making Applications to Church Planting

The Bangkok team continually considered applications that might flow from their research findings. They did so with the perspective of envisioning. What might the church look like among the people groups of Bangkok? As discussed earlier in this manual, envisioning is a perspective that permeates all of Caleb Project Research.

In Bangkok, the team used their research findings to make suggestions about church planting. One application had to do with culturally relevant leadership in the church. The team found that even when *Thai-teh* join a church, one of the primary reasons they subsequently leave has to do with leadership patterns in the church. Among the Chinese, leadership is something to which one aspires. A leader is a strong, self-motivated, entrepreneurial, and visionary. Among the Thai, by contrast, a leader is someone who is self-effacing, who only steps forward to lead when the group insists upon it. To the Chinese, the Thai appear lazy and uninterested in leadership. To the Thai, the Chinese appear pushy and interested only in power and prestige, rather than service.

Since most churches are Chinese, the Chinese are generally blind to the fact that leadership style is an issue as far as the Thais are concerned. Thais don't feel comfortable in churches run by people who lead in the manner of the Chinese and they are unlikely to become active members in Chinese churches. So what would a Thai-oriented church look like? What leadership model should its leaders follow? The Bangkok team's final research report entitled *Reaching the Peoples of Bangkok* makes some suggestions.

The Bangkok team members spent a lot of time during their third month on the field drafting their research report. They tried to summarize what they had learned and to confirm the things of which they weren't quite sure. They also used their research to write a slide show script and a prayer guide. Then they took photographs to illustrate these projects. These became tools for mobilizing the church once they returned to the United States.

Return to the States

After twelve weeks on the field, the team returned to the United States for team debrief (see page 157). They tried to unwind from their high-intensity cross-cultural experience. They also completed a slide show and prayer guide about Bangkok. The research coordinator finished their research report a few months after team debrief ended.

The Bangkok team made a presentation of their slide show and prayer guide to practice mobilizing before they returned to their homes. Some left considering whether or not they might return to Bangkok as church planters. Others became spokesmen for the people whose needs they had researched. (See Appendix III: People Specific Advocacy on page 171.)

The Bangkok case study highlights the lifecycle of a typical Caleb Project Research Expedition. It gives a brief example of how a research team begins, proceeds, and comes to an end. Four aspects of a successful research team also merit a deeper look. These are team leadership, practice research, team debrief, and mobilization tools.

Team Leadership

Pastor and Pilot: The Team Leader

We value excellent leadership, so we are committed to recruiting high caliber leaders and to equipping them for their role on our teams. But what responsibilities are given to a team leader? What qualifications must he or she possess to fulfill those responsibilities? How are team leaders trained? These questions will be answered in the following section.

Team Leader Responsibilities

Caleb Project entrusts the pastoral care of team members and the logistics of living and working overseas to the team leader. As pastor and pilot, a team leader's daily responsibilities are varied. Some tasks are miserably mundane such as making sure the landlord sprayed for fleas. Others require crisis intervention, like counseling a team member who is ready to hop a cab to the airport.

For Caleb Project Research Expeditions, team leader responsibilities have been entrusted to men and not to women. This choice has risen from the difficulties women face getting things done in cultures where they are not accepted as leaders. By referring to team leaders as men in the remainder of this section, we are not implying that women cannot be used by God as leaders in other overseas situations.

Team leaders are called upon to guide team members in completing an intensive project. Their myriad responsibilities can be divided into survival tasks, people tasks, and logistical tasks.

Survival tasks

These things must be done by the team leader for his own development and to protect his personal well-being. If team leaders do not take care of themselves, they cannot care for their teams.

> ***Prayer:*** The team leader must protect time for personal communion with God through prayer and Bible study.

Delegation: The team leader must actively delegate any roles and jobs that he does not need to do himself.

Personal development: The team leader must take time to consider what God is teaching him and how he is being changed by God through his experience.

People tasks

The most important role of a team leader is that of pastor. He is entrusted for the duration of the expedition with the emotional and spiritual welfare of his team members. While we do not expect our team leaders to solve team member's problems, we do expect him to listen and carefully respond to the issues that are thrilling or haunting them. A team leader's people-oriented tasks fall into three basic categories: leading the charge, shepherding the flock, and coaching the team.

Leading the charge

The team leader sets the tempo and models a proper attitude for the team to follow. He may inspire vision and commitment when morale is down or rekindle zeal when it is flagging. A team leader's faith will be tested and stretched in doing so. Individuals, and sometimes whole teams, have faced crisis points over the course of a research expedition. Sometimes the survival of a team depends on the team leader's ability to hear God's voice and communicate his direction to the team.

One day during an expedition to India, a Caleb Project team was caught up in a religious mob of over half a million people. As the crowd pressed in and swept them along, the women on the team were pinched, prodded, and otherwise touched in inappropriate ways. Looking around for an escape route, they fought a growing sense of panic. They were unfamiliar with the city and the crowd seemed to stretch for miles down every street they passed. In desperation, the men on the team began swinging their arms to clear a path for the women. Soon a young Indian boy, seeing their fear, caught the team's attention and escorted them through a maze of back alleys away from the crowd until they could find their way home.

In silence the team walked up the steps leading into the guest house where they were staying. The women felt dazed and horrified. They struggled to fight a growing sense of revulsion toward a culture whose people treat women so horribly. The men were shaken as well, fearful and saddened by what had happened. Later that evening, the team leader sat on the balcony of the guest house crying, asking God if the team could continue, if they could weather this storm. He considered giving up and taking the team home. He wondered if an error on his part had led his team into this situation. As God reminded him of the things he had done to bring the team to this point, the team leader felt his faith strengthened. He received confidence to press on and to pull the team together. As the team prayed, God gave them courage to face their fear and anger. He reminded them of his great love for the people of India.

The team chose to stay and carry out their work, trusting God to give them love for the men who abused them. Strong, faith-filled leadership was essential for the team to come through such a difficult situation.

Shepherding the flock

A team leader's primary thought, energy, and prayer is dedicated to caring for the members of his team. Their success, safety, and growth should be his foremost concern. From the beginning of team training to the end of team debrief, we encourage our team leaders to shepherd their flock. During training they build relationships with their team members. They try to understand the fears and hopes that each individual brings to the project. Once overseas, the team leader continues to grow in relationship with his team. He helps them deal with culture stress, with team conflicts, and encourages spiritual growth. As the team prepares to return home, the team leader helps individuals consider their future role in missions. How they will steward what God has given them through their overseas experience?

We encourage our team leaders to carry out their shepherding responsibilities in both informal and formal ways. Team leaders should always be on the lookout for ways to encourage their team. They should show interest in the progress each team member makes, and model a way of relating that others can follow.

In addition, team leaders meet formally with each team member at least once every two weeks. An hour is set aside to talk privately. During this more formal time, the team leader tries to listen and help team members think about any problems they may be facing. Culture stress is often a topic of conversation. Cross-cultural experience on the part of the team leader is quite valuable at this point. Having faced many of the same feelings his team members have, he can assure them that they are not alone. Understanding is a starting point for many people in processing their feelings of culture stress.

A sensitive team leader listens actively and thoroughly to the feelings team members share. He helps them think about how to respond to their feelings. A team leader who shares his own struggles and solicits opinions and advice regarding the progress of the team may find team members growing in their responsiveness over time.

One-on-ones, as we call these formal shepherding times, are also valuable for mobilizing team members. A leader can ask thought provoking questions regarding team members' missions experience. He can help them consider what role God might have for them in the future.

Coaching the team

A final people task that team leaders have is assigning team members to various roles and jobs. (Team member roles are further explained in Appendix IV, page 173). Some roles, such as worship leader and treasurer last through the entire project. Other tasks may be short-term or passed from one team member to the next. While coaching a team, leaders face familiar challenges: maximizing the abilities of their people and inspiring team members to do things that no one wants to do.

Logistical tasks

Team leaders oversee logistical details in five main areas. In each area we encourage our leaders to delegate as many details as possible.

Communication

We ask that teams report to the Caleb Project members within 72 hours of arrival in their host city. After that, we expect to be updated once a week. The team leader uses each report to tell us how team members are doing and how we can pray for them. Even though the team leader prepares each report, a team member can see that reports are delivered. Teams have used faxes, electronic mail, or regular post to communicate with our office.

Finance

The team leader is responsible for the team's money and how it is spent. Working with the team treasurer, the leader monitors the budget and anticipates upcoming expenses. He also makes financial decisions regarding housing and travel to other parts of the country.

Scheduling

Team leaders, working with their research coordinators, design a schedule for their entire project. They establish a daily and weekly routine, plan times for team travel and homestays, and make sure that various projects progress on schedule. Team leaders should be sensitive to the pace and fatigue level of their team and provide extra time off when it is needed. At other times, teams need encouragement to keep up a good pace.

Scheduling becomes particularly important as teams near the end of their time

*Five to seven days are set
aside for a vacation.*

report of their research findings. Others will be frantically chasing down elusive bits of research information. Everyone wants to finish last minute souvenir shopping and say good-bye to friends.

Travel

Caleb Project researchers usually live in a single city for three months with the exception of two travel times. Five to seven days are set aside for a vacation. The team leader arranges for travel to a relaxing place where the team can rest and regroup. Everyone enjoys a break from the hustle and bustle of the city and from an intense research schedule.

Teams also spend four to seven days visiting other parts of the country to benefit their research. They travel in small groups to other cities or villages to gain a broader perspective. Again, the team leader is responsible for scheduling and making arrangements for this travel.

Security

Finally, the team leader helps serve as a security watchdog. This is important in countries which are hostile to the spread of the gospel. For security reasons, the team leader, rather than team members, may interview expatriate workers and Christian converts. He advises the team about researching volatile minority groups and warns the team of questions that should be avoided. Another security issue is how open the team can be in sharing their faith with cultural helpers.

Team Leader Qualifications

The responsibilities we expect team leaders to carry out determine the qualifications they need. In summary, we want team leaders to have the following qualifications:

- Previous leadership experience

- Previous cross-cultural experience

- A heart for mobilizing team members

Please refer to the team leader profile in Appendix IV for more details on team leader qualifications.

Team Leader Training

Team leaders participate in an additional week of training prior to the arrival of their team. During their training, we lay a foundation of values and principles that enable team leaders to make decisions on the field. We recognize that we cannot predict every situation team leaders may face. Instead of attempting this, we outline team leader responsibilities and potential pitfalls they may face. Then we equip leaders by giving them biblical principles for effective leadership. This training is usually presented by previous Caleb Project Research Expedition team leaders.

Leadership Pitfalls

To conclude this section on team leaders we will consider leadership pitfalls. These two issues have proven to be struggles for many of our leaders.

Leadership Responsibilities vs. Research Responsibilities

Team leaders face difficulty when they attempt to do as much research as team members while being faithful to their leadership responsibilities. These leaders need to find a better balance so that they do not become emotionally, mentally, and physically exhausted. On the other hand, team leaders can fill their days without ever giving time to the team's research. Team members may question why they have to "do all the work themselves."

Each team leader is different, but we advise them to place priority on leadership tasks, and then to spend time researching. Team leaders should do *some* research because we believe that leading by example is important.

Loneliness

Team leaders, particularly single ones, have also struggled with loneliness. This stress is lessened when their team members support them in emotional and practical ways.

Leading a Caleb Project Research Expedition exacts a toll on the hardiest men. However, God has often used this leadership experience in significant ways. Most team leaders have finished their expeditions with a deepened sense of dependence on God and a greater confidence that he will continue to use them in his kingdom.

Navigator and Dispatcher:
The Research Coordinator

A second leadership role on Caleb Project Research Expeditions is that of research coordinator. Research coordinators are facilitators who help set directions for the team's research. We created the research coordinator role so that team leaders could focus primarily on pastoral and logistical tasks. While the team leader carries out these responsibilities, the research coordinator navigates in the sea of cultural learning and dispatches researchers to explore the city. We want to note here that though our team leaders have been men, most of our research coordinators have been women.

Research Coordinator Responsibilities

Research coordinators face high degrees of ambiguity. No one knows exactly how the research will progress. This makes leading the team's research step by step practically impossible. However, research coordinators can provide leadership that facilitates the research. They can help team members feel confident and able to carry out research tasks.

Research coordinators cultivate an atmosphere where there is freedom to risk – to try and sometimes to fail. Their availability, patience, and constant affirmation is invaluable to the team as they set out together on a grand adventure.

Preparing

Caleb Project research coordinators often prepare for their role by gathering written materials on their target city or people group. They read a lot. As much as possible, they sift through information to develop a research focus. Networking with mission agencies, national workers, and others can be invaluable for preparing research coordinators to succeed in their role.

Making teamlet assignments

A first step upon arrival overseas is to make teamlet assignments. Given the team's research goals, research coordinators choose topics and assign them to team members so that they can focus their interviews with cultural helpers.

For example, most research projects begin by examining social stratification. Research coordinators pick topics that will shed light on stratification and send team members out to track on those topics. Who researches with whom, who researches what, and how long teamlets track on topics are all decisions that research coordinators make.

Relating to cultural helpers

Research coordinators help the team keep track of cultural helpers. An important aspect of any research project is making sure that you are studying a good representation of the society. Cultural helpers are needed from all levels of society. While we do not monitor our cultural helper pool according to academic standards, we do evaluate it. If needed, research coordinators can encourage team members to pursue new and different contacts. Research coordinators can help team members evaluate their interaction with cultural helpers. Are they good helpers? Is impression management occurring?

For the sake of organization, research coordinators keep a running list of cultural helper's names, addresses, and phone numbers. This list is invaluable when the team wants to fill in certain gaps in their research.

Each week, research coordinators facilitate group discussion about the research.

Writing Notes

The skill of writing fieldnotes and filenotes develops over time. For some team members it comes naturally, but others need encouragement and help from research coordinators to learn this skill. The "So What?" and "What Now?" portions of filenotes are particularly important. Research coordinators can give teammates feedback on these sections to stimulate better analysis and missiological thinking.

Good opportunities for giving feedback are strategy meetings, or informal times when team members write their filenotes. Like team leaders, research coordinators often take time to meet one-on-one, every other week, with team members. During these meetings, research coordinators encourage team members and help them develop their research skills.

Leading strategy meetings

Each week, research coordinators facilitate group discussion about the research. These strategy meetings require a certain amount of preparation and direction from research coordinators.

All the filenotes generated from a week's interviews should be read by the team before strategy meetings. Research coordinators may ask team members to read for different topics or to lead a portion of the group discussion. Enough time is needed for reading filenotes before strategy meetings begin.

Group discussions can be invigorating, frustrating, inspiring, and overwhelming, but they are essential. The main responsibilities of research coordinators during a strategy meeting is to draw out the team's ideas about what they learned during the week. They also help teams decide what to research next and arrange teamlets and topic assignments to do research effectively.

A general strategy meeting agenda might include the following:

- *Feedback from the research coordinator*

- *A short review, if needed*

- *Presentation of research findings*

- *Group discussion of findings to interpret their meaning and apply them to the work of church planting*

- *Gathering topics and questions for the coming week*

- *Assigning new teamlet partners and research topics*

- *Teamlet partners discussing their research plan and specific questions for the coming week*

Setting a pace

Research teams need to pace themselves so that their research can be completed in the time allotted. Research coordinators, in cooperation with team leaders, play a role in setting that pace. Broadly, research coordinators keep end goals in mind, making sure that all areas of research interest are covered. They help the team move from one stage of research to the next.

More specifically, research coordinators look at all the possibilities, at their teammates, and at their project goals to make schedules and plans for completing the research. There are many choices to be made. For example, will team members spend time staying in homes with their cultural helpers, traveling to other parts of the country, or vacationing? When should the team begin writing about their research findings? If staff members from Caleb Project come to visit the team, how should the team utilize them?

Making writing assignments

Research coordinators are responsible for seeing that the research goals are met. This often includes writing a final research report. Caleb Project researchers share writing responsibilities and research coordinators facilitate and oversee the process. They make writing assignments and help researchers communicate the team's findings in the best possible way. After the team generates a writing outline, research coordinators make assignments and choose realistic writing deadlines. While some team members specialize in writing, others may continue researching. Each group will continue to need the research coordinator's guidance.

Monitoring security

In research settings where teams need to take extra security precautions, research coordinators share responsibility with team leaders for this. They may limit the team's contact with expatriate workers, national Christians, and converts. They decide what books and articles are safe to take into the country and then take care that filenotes are not thrown away, lost, or left lying around.

Wrapping up

Most Caleb Project research coordinators continue to work on final research reports after teams have returned to their homes. They write final drafts and see that strategy reports are completed and distributed.

Research Coordinator Qualifications

Many Caleb Project research coordinators have participated in previous expeditions as team members. Whether they have this experience or not, we feel that the most important qualification for coordinating the research is good group participation skills. The ability to facilitate a group project is more important than research or missions expertise.

Facilitating the research requires good listening skills, the ability to seek out information, and to summarize findings. Research coordinators should be confident with people and be able to inspire each team member to contribute their best to the task. Organizational skills are also very important.

Because research coordinators write strategy reports, they should also be confident writers who can communicate clearly and concisely. To do so, they will need to understand their team's research findings and how those findings can be applied to the work of church planting.

Research Coordinator Training

Caleb Project provides a week of leadership training for both team leaders and research coordinators. A portion of this training focuses on the responsibilities of the research coordinator. All other elements of training are the same as those described for team leaders.

Team leaders and research coordinators discuss together their various responsibilities in light of biblical leadership values and principles. As they do so, they begin to work out a style and plan for working together as leaders. As joint team leaders, they must work in tandem – understanding each other's roles and encouraging one another to carry them out for the benefit of their team members.

Research coordinators have unique opportunities to facilitate their team's research even before going overseas. The following section describes practical training for the entire team. During these practice opportunities, research coordinators use their navigational abilities so that they too can develop their skills in leading the team's research.

Practice Research Opportunities

A young man scurried down a street in New York City with a violin case tucked under his arm and paused to ask directions to his destination. He approached a well dressed man standing at a corner, and inquired, "Could you tell me, sir, how do I get to Carnegie Hall?" The man looked at him and replied, "Practice, practice, practice."

The best way to learn how to do research is to practice doing it. While *Exploring the Land* gives a lot of practical advice – and other resources are available – you just have to *do* research to see how everything works together.

Objectives for practice research should be:

- To work as a team. The whole group learns to work together, and each member learns to work with various partners to interview and record notes.

- To gain exposure to cross-cultural issues. Team members learn to interact, to speak, and to listen across cultural barriers. Team members begin to feel comfortable moving about in different cultures.

- To practice aspects of research. Team members grow in their ability to initiate conversations, to ask questions in the course of an ethnographic interview, to take fieldnotes and write filenotes, and to judge good and bad cultural helpers.

- To adapt to the pace of the project. Practice events help team members recognize the diligence and hard work required for the success of the project.

- To expose team members to experienced researchers. Caleb Project Research Expeditions make extensive use of coaches. These staff and former team members model effective interviewing techniques and offer constructive criticism of team members' work.

- To gain confidence in researching and a sense of felt need for training. Practicing helps team members realize that they can, in fact, discover important cultural information through interviewing. It also makes them aware that there is much they still need to learn.

Caleb Project Research Expedition training usually includes three different practice experiences. While role playing is often employed in the course of lectures, these three research events actually take team members out on the street to meet strangers, ask questions, and record their findings.

Scavenger Hunt: Cross-cultural Foray

Early on in training, often within the first week, team members are sent in groups of twos and threes on a scavenger hunt to an ethnic neighborhood. They try to answer questions by carefully observing and by initiating conversations with people who live or work in the neighborhood. For example, the team might go to

Chinatown and try to locate *dim sum*, to purchase a medicinal herb, and to begin at least three conversations with shop keepers.

The scavenger hunt is designed to set a tone for the research project. It communicates that our research is done on the street, not in an office, library, or classroom. Team members who have had little cross-cultural exposure begin to feel comfortable in such contexts. They return after two or three hours and talk about their experience.

International Student Experience:
Cross-cultural Exploration

Midway through training, a day is given to conducting interviews with international students. We arrange for team members to meet students at a nearby university or community college. Instructors who teach English as a second language have often allowed our team members to interview their students.

Before this practice session, specific instruction about asking questions and making records of research findings is given. Caleb Project trainers, or team research coordinators, give team members specific topics to pursue. Teamlet partners practice interviewing and take notes of their conversation with an international student. They practice building rapport with cultural helpers and pursue themes by asking a variety of descriptive, structural, and contrast questions. After the prearranged class time, team members practice "trolling" on campus to locate other foreigners to talk to. Then they write filenotes using the format they have learned. Ample time is given to debriefing this experience.

Team leaders facilitate this debrief by asking questions about what the team learned and about feelings associated with their practice research experience. Research coordinators review filenotes and give helpful feedback to their team.

Field Practice: Cross-cultural Immersion

The fourth week of Caleb Project Research Expedition training is spent in a foreign city. When our offices were located in Los Angeles, teams went to Tijuana, Mexico. Now that we are located in Denver, teams conduct field practice in Juarez, Mexico. Many of our alumni have said that their field practice experience was the most significant part of their training. Five days in Mexico make four weeks in the classroom come to life.

The field practice emulates an entire project, but it is compressed into just five days. Team members live, eat, and worship together. With the help of their research coordinator, they set a focus for their research. Then they spend time on the street, meeting cultural helpers and conducting interviews. Evenings are given to writing filenotes and discussing what is learned. Two mini-strategy meetings are led by the research coordinator as well. One morning is spent prayerwalking. During the last evening team members write a brief research report.

Team members experience many of the things they will face overseas such as the joys and trials of living and working as a team. They begin to learn how to get along and conduct research in a foreign culture. Total immersion is a key to the usefulness of this experience. If at all possible, take your team out of their home culture prior to going to your target city.

Compressing a twelve-week project into five days in Mexico has drawbacks. Relationships with nationals are rushed and it is difficult to give attention to building rapport, especially when you only have a few days in the city. The validity of the information the team obtains is also reduced. Even with these drawbacks, practical lessons can be learned through the experience.

Finally, take sufficient time to thoroughly debrief the field practice. We usually spend five to six hours discussing what happened, how the team felt about the experience, what they learned, and reinforcing various research skills.

Conclusion

These practice experiences have been tried and tested by Caleb Project researchers. There certainly may be other ways to practice. The main goal is for team members to put into action the theory they learned in the classroom. The American composer John Cage once mused, "All I know about method is that when I am not working I sometimes think I know something, but when I am working, it is quite clear I know nothing." It is better for team members to realize this before they go to live among the people they intend to research.

Team Debrief

A unique characteristic of our short-term missions experience is the emphasis we place on debriefing teams. Caleb Project Research teams spend three weeks together in the United States following their twelve weeks overseas. This segment of the project, which we call team debrief, serves as a buffer between the overseas adventure and returning home. While the first couple of days are usually set aside for rest and recovery from jet lag, the remainder of the time is scheduled to accomplish three main objectives. These objectives are:

- *To help team members process their experience*

- *To prepare team members to move on with their lives*

- *To produce mobilization tools*

Processing the Experience

For most people, living overseas, even for a short time, results in monumental life change. Perspectives are broadened, assumptions are washed away, and in some cases, these changes are traumatic. Team members benefit the most from their experience when they can successfully integrate these changes into their lives. Debrief helps that integration begin. Significant changes cannot be totally processed in three weeks. Our desire, however, is for issues to be identified and for contemplation to begin. We see a need for people to process their experience on at least four levels:

- *In relation to themselves. Team members should be encouraged to write and talk about the changes God has brought to their lives. Little will bring sin to the surface of someone's life like living in a team setting in another culture. God often causes growth, changing wrong attitudes, and ways of relating to others.*

- *In relation to the team. Because a root of bitterness in someone's life can taint the experience for years, Caleb Project researchers are given time to resolve conflicts that have risen on the team. They are encouraged to go to others on the team whom they have offended to seek forgiveness.*

- *In relation to Caleb Project. We also give team members an opportunity to evaluate their experience with us. They evaluate themselves, their team leader and research coordinator, and Caleb Project. They comment on the effectiveness of training and the overall value of the research expedition.*

- *In relation to God. Researchers also process their attitudes to God and his sovereignty. Ministering in an unreached situation can cause even the most mature to question the status of the lost and to wonder why God hasn't done something. We want to allow team members to be honest about what they are feeling and to ask the tough questions they are wrestling with.*

Preparing to Go Home

The second major purpose of team debrief is preparing team members to return home. We have joked, "Once a Caleb Project researcher, always a Caleb Project researcher." In reality, we do want the impact of a Caleb Project Research Expedition to be lifelong. For that to happen, team members may need to deal with reverse culture shock, home life, stewardship, and other integration issues.

Reverse Culture Shock

For many people reintegrating into their home culture is more difficult than going into a new culture. Things that for years have been assumed, are now seen in a different light. The dissonance caused by this, particularly when team members have looked forward to coming home with great longing, can be excruciating. Some face this pain by forgetting their time overseas as soon as possible, essentially boxing it up and relegating it to the past. Others, still in the honeymoon glow of their guest culture, will turn on their home culture, decrying its materialism, its self-absorption, and its carnal spiritual state. Both of these responses rob team members of the best fruit of their experience. Both also severely limit their ability to talk with others – one through inactivity, the other by offending those who listen to them.

We want to help our team members deal successfully with reverse culture shock. To do so they need time to assess how they are feeling, they need to be advised about what to expect, and they need to be reassured that what they are experiencing is normal.

Reentering home life

Many team members return to home situations that are extremely challenging. Almost all are surprised to find that friends and family are not as interested in their trip as they are. This can precipitate feelings of sadness and betrayal. We encourage team members to think about and prepare for their home situations. We also provide some practical tips for dealing with difficult situations.

Stewarding their experience

Remembering Jesus's words that "to whom much is given, much will be required," we want to equip our team members to be good stewards of what God has given them through their research expedition. We want them to consider what their responsibility might be to the people they have researched. "Should I return as a church planter to these people?" "How can I encourage others to care for these people and equip intercessors to pray for the unreached?" Believing that effective mobilization is crucial to proper stewardship, we take time during debrief to train team members to be effective mobilizers.

Integrating the expedition into life

Finally, we want our team members to consider how this experience fits in with the rest of their lives. Far too many people compartmentalize and shelve significant experiences. Each event is viewed as an end in itself. Rather, we want Caleb Project Research Expeditions to be a step in the journey down which God is leading each team member. We want them to recognize how their lives have led up to the expedition and how the expedition leads them to their next stage of life and beyond. We facilitate this type of integration by leading team members through times of reflective and prayerful life processing.

Producing Mobilization Tools

The production of mobilization tools will be addressed in detail in the following section, but one point should be discussed here. A difficulty we have faced during team debrief is balancing the production of mobilization tools and the debriefing of team members, while trying to provide sufficient rest for the team. Because of this, we have expanded debrief for Caleb Project Research Expeditions from ten hours to three weeks.

When the team returns, a couple days of solid rest are scheduled. These days of rest are followed by an intense time of mobilization tool production with a limited number of debrief sessions. In order to send finished mobilization tools home with team members, most of the work on these projects must be completed by the middle of the second week of debrief. After the midpoint of debrief, when most materials have gone to the printer, we shift the focus from tool production to personal reflection. If all goes well, the schedule lightens for most team members during the last days of team debrief.

Mobilization Tools

God has given Caleb Project a mandate to mobilize the Church to complete world evangelization. Our research teams fulfill this mandate primarily through the growth that takes place in team members' lives. They are filled with a vision to see the church planted among all peoples. In addition, they are equipped to think

Media tools are developed during the expedition which team members use to communicate God's heart for the people they researched.

and act in new ways. Some build on their research experience and return to places where peoples have yet to be reached with the gospel.

Caleb Project also fulfills this mobilization mandate by equipping team members to be effective mobilizers. We want researchers to bring back to their constituency, like Caleb and Joshua, a good report of the land. To that end, media tools are developed during the expedition which team members use to communicate God's heart for the people they researched.

Mobilization tools, as these media projects are called, help team members convey the significance of their experience. Using the combined insight and vision of the whole team, high quality prayer guides and videos present interesting, brief, and focused information on the work of God among the unreached. Sometimes additional mobilization tools have been produced. See *Appendix II: Caleb Project Resources* on page 167 for a complete list of our mobilization tools.

Team members use these materials to introduce specific unreached peoples to those they hope to mobilize. Interested listeners can purchase prayer guides and videos from Caleb Project's Resource department. Team members can also mail prayer guides and videos to friends and supporters who are far away.

Prayer guides and videos are also sent out from the Caleb Project office on a continual basis to mobilize people beyond the team member's constituency. Missionaries, churches, and agencies that we have networked with about the research are usually eager to use our mobilization tools. A great need exists for first-hand reports on unreached peoples and we have seen our mobilization tools be used broadly. Much prayer has been mobilized for previously unknown peoples.

Producing Mobilization Tools

We cannot give you a complete guide to producing effective mobilization tools – that would take too much time and space. However, a brief explanation of the production plan we follow may be worthwhile. What must be done during training, during the research, and during team debrief to finish quality mobilization tools?

During Team Training

During team training three things about mobilization tools should be established. First, the team should consider the audience they hope to mobilize. Understanding their audience helps the team answer the next question. What tools should be produced? Some limitations will guide this decision. The team only has a certain amount of money, time, and skill. Given these parameters, the team decides the best mobilization tools to produce and how many they can afford. Finally, the team leader assigns a captain and working group to each tool the team decides to create.

During the Research

Teams keep mobilization tools in mind while doing their research. As early as the second or third week in-country, teams begin to spend a half day a week working on mobilization tools. They plan their work so that they have solid second drafts of their projects ready when they return for team debrief.

Quality pictures must be taken. As soon as an outline for a prayer guide and a script for a video comes together, a team photographer begins shooting the needed photographs. A photographer will get more appropriate shots when he is shooting for a finished script and a specific photo list. He or she will also do better when they know more about the city and have better friends to photograph. However, if photographers wait too long, they may find themselves compromised by the constraints of waning time.

Two important points regarding photography should be mentioned.

- *Whenever possible, have a visiting staff member carry film home for early processing. If slides are ready to be examined when the team returns, many valuable hours can be saved.*

As soon as an outline for a prayer guide and a script for a video comes together, a team photographer begins shooting the needed photographs.

- *Taking pictures of believers and workers in high security situations can devastate the work of the gospel there. Caleb Project operates according to a policy which forbids both taking or using such photographs.*

During Team Debrief

Team debrief is a busy time. Each day of the three weeks buzzes with focused activity. Prayer guides go to press and videos are completed. In the rush of deadlines and the heat of production, time for team leaders to care for the spiritual and emotional needs of team members must be guarded. It is better for team members to return home having processed their feelings than having finished their mobilization tools.

With this priority in mind, we try to do two things with tool production during team debrief.

- *We work according to a production schedule so that, if at all possible, team members can take completed projects home with them.*

- *We make sure each project is reviewed by a staff editor. We carry organizational responsibility for the content of prayer guides and videos. We cannot allow the pressure of dead-lines to cause us to abdicate this responsibility. It is better for a project to be delayed than for it to contain information that will have to be retracted later.*

Conclusion

I have written you quite boldly on some points, as if to remind you of them again, because of the grace God gave me to be a minister of Christ Jesus to the Gentiles with the priestly duty of proclaiming the gospel of God, so that the Gentiles might become an offering acceptable to God, sanctified by the Holy Spirit (Romans 15:15-16).

In this passage, Paul celebrates his calling to offer Gentile nations to God as acceptable sacrifices. We at Caleb Project share Paul's joy at the privilege of offering the nations to God. We believe that our research is a small but important component of a holy and complex process. This process begins with an unreached people and ends with a band of joyous worshippers from among them. As you apply this research method, you join thousands of saints from throughout history and from around the world who have sought God's heart for the establishment of the Church among all peoples.

May God anoint your efforts to understand the unique glory he has designed into the people who have won your heart. As you study and question and pray, may he unfold before you a rich and detailed picture of their culture. May he grant you eyes to see what their church will look like. How might they reflect God's glory while fully embracing their culture as they become enfolded into the worldwide body of Christ?

Along the way, should you have questions, need help, or simply want to share your story, feel free to contact Caleb Project. With you, we are longing for that day when some from every nation, tribe, and tongue will gather before God's throne and, at last, offer the praise and honor of which he is worthy.

Appendix I:
What is Caleb Project?

At Penn State University in 1980, four young men were so moved by a vision to win the world for Christ that they decided to prove a point. If they could minister for a year in Libya, the most militant Muslim country on earth, they would demonstrate that no country on earth is closed to the gospel. They intended to return with a call for others to join them in seeing the world evangelized, even in the most difficult and uninviting situations.

Twenty-four other students committed to support the four pioneers with prayer and encouragement. All those involved signed a pledge to devote their entire lives to make disciples of all nations, "wherever and however God leads, giving priority to the peoples currently beyond the reach of the gospel." This pledge became known as the Caleb Declaration.

After a year in Libya, the four returned to challenge other students to involvement. Their model was Caleb, who returned from the promised land to challenge his fellow Israelites to "by all means go up and take possession of the land ... the Lord is with us" (Numbers 13:30,14:9, NASB).

More than two decades later, Caleb Project continues to challenge believers to be involved in world evangelization, by going into the "promised land," by helping to equip and send others, and by praying for the accomplishment of God's purposes.

Caleb Project focuses attention on the least-evangelized people groups of the world and mobilizes Christians to reach them.

Caleb Project offers a wide array of tools and services that connect individuals, churches, and other ministries to God's work among unreached peoples.

- *Carefully researched videos, prayer guides, ethnographic reports, and other materials to enhance missions awareness and encourage informed prayer for the unreached.*

- *Short-term trips among unreached peoples to bring Christians face-to-face with the needs of the unreached.*

- *The life-changing* Perspectives on the World Christian Movement *and* Perspectives on the World of Islam *courses.*

- *Professional speakers and trainers to rally local churches, challenge college students, and prepare children for effective ministry on behalf of the unreached.*

- *Training seminars, electronic forums, and helpful resources to encourage Christians to champion the needs of specific unreached people groups.*

Appendix II:
Caleb Project Resources

Ethnographic Resources

Research Expedition Strategy Reports:

These reports are based on research expeditions done in the years indicated. Please contact Caleb Project Resources at 303.730.4182 for details on how to order these. All other resources listed can be purchased at *www.calebproject.org*.

Strategy Reports Available

Achanese, Sumatra Indonesia (1993)
Adana, Turkey (1990)
Alexandria, Egypt (1984)
Azerbaijanis, Azerbaijan (1995)
Baluch of Karchi, Pakistan (1985)
Banias, North India (to be completed 2003)
Bangkok, Thailand (1988)
Bombay Muslims, India (1988)
Calcutta Muslims, India (1990)
Dai, China (to be completed 2003)
Damascus, Syria (1990)
Delhi Muslims, India (1988)
Delhi Squatters, India (1985)

Irbid's Muslims (1987)
Istanbul, Turkey (1986)
Kazakhs, Kazakhstan (1992)
Madurese, Indonesia (1997)
Patna Muslims, India (1990)
Rajput, India (2002)
Sikhs of the Punjab, India (to be completed 2003)
Sourashtras, South India (1985)
Turkmen, Turkmenistan (1994)
Malay, urban, Malaysia (1988)
Uzbeks, Uzbeksitan (1992)

Field & Research Related Titles

Keys to the Nations (Explanded Edition). Item #01-0301. Book. This popular revised title is a comprehensive compilation of articles written by seasoned missions experts on unreached peoples. Topics covered include understanding unreached peoples, establishing effective partnerships to reach a people, facilitating people group adoption, maintaining security, and fundraising among others. It is an invaluable tool in unlocking the doors to the nations! (261 pages, 2002).

Pioneer Church Planting: A Rookie Team Leader's Handbook. Item #01-0302. Workbook. Compiled by overseas church planters, this book includes valuable guidance in the following areas: basic requirements for team leaders, screening and assessing of candidates, preparation of new team members, research, networking strategies, articulation of ministry philosophy, and much more! (98 pages, 2001).

Prayer Journeys: A Leader's How-To Manual. Item #01-0303. Book. A great resource for church groups or individuals wishing to make the best of their time on a missions trip among unreached peoples. Learn practical ways to prepare, both physically and spiritually, to be more effective. (70 pages, 1995).

Unreached People Group Booklets. These booklets are designed so that the reader may understand the cultures of the people groups covered, how one might become involved in seeing them reached, and to enable the reader to pray effectively for them. The booklets are typically 24-36 pages. The majority of these booklets have come from the teams that have done research among unreached people groups upon completion of their research trip.

Booklets with a companion video (available separately) are marked with an asterisk (*).

Ansari: India* (2000) #02-0424
Azerbaijanis: Azerbaijan (1995) #02-0403
Chantik Muslims: Indonesia (1993) #02-0437
Dai: China (2002) #02-0442
Dungan: Kyrgystan (2001) #02-0437
Kazaks: China (2002) #02-0439
Kazakhs: Kazakhstan* (2000) #02-0415
Kyrgyz & Dungan: Kyrgystan* (1996) #02-0427
Madurese: Indonesia* (1996) #02-0429
Muslims of Patna: India (1990) #02-0416
Rajputs: India* (2000) #02-0434
Riffi Berbers: Morocco (1998) #02-0420
Sikhs: India* (2001)#02-0423
Tibetans (general): China (1999) #02-0440
Tibetans, Kham: China* (2000) #02-0428
Turks: Turkey* (1997) #02-0425
Turkmen: Turkmenistan (2001) #02-0419
Uyghurs: China & Kazakhstan (2000) #02-0441
Uzbeks: Uzbekistan* (revised 2002) #02-0430

Unreached People Group Videos. Each video cassette contains both a short and long version – approximately 3 minutes and 18 minutes in length – and is designed for viewing in congregations or smaller group settings. Caleb Project's videos are unique in that the majority of these videos were shot during a research expedition, so the viewer gets an insider's view of these unreached peoples!

Videos with a companion People Group Booklet are marked with an asterisk (*).

Ansari: India* (2001) #02-0124, PAL #02-0224
Fulani: Burkina Faso (2001) #02-0107, PAL #02-0237, Extended Length #02-0307
Kazakhs: Kazakhstan* (1999) #02-0115, PAL #02-0215
Kyrgyz & Dungan: Kyrgystan* (1996) #02-0127, PAL #02-0227
Madurese: Indonesia* (1996) #02-0129, PAL #02-0229
Malay: Malaysia & Singapore; #02-0131, PAL #02-0231
Maratha: India (1997) #02-0132, PAL #02-0232
Miao/Hmong: China (2000) #02-0133, PAL #02-0233
Rajputs: India* (2000) #02-0134, PAL #02-0234
Riffi Berbers: Morocco (1998) #02-0120, PAL #02-0220
Sikhs: India* (2002) #02-0123, PAL #02-0223
Sumatran Malay: Malaysia (2002) #02-0136, PAL #02-0236
Tajiks: Central Asia (1999) #02-0122, PAL #02-0222
Tatars, Volga: Tatarstan (1999) #02-0135, PAL #02-0235
Tibetans, Amdo: China (1996) #02-0126, PAL #02-0226
Tibetans, Kham: China* (2000) #02-0128, PAL #02-0228
Turks: Turkey (1997) #02-0125, PAL #02-0225
Uzbeks: Uzbekistan* (1998) #02-0130, PAL #02-0230

Unreached People Group Slide Shows.
Azerbaijanis (1995) #02-0103
Turkmen (1994) #02-0119

Other Caleb Project Resources

- Mobilization Tools. These products are designed to help you mobilize individuals and groups towards involvement with unreached peoples. Tools include *Missions Skits – Dramas and Skits that Mobilize*, *Perspectives* promo videos, and more!

- Life Guidance Products. Tools such as *God's Heart for the Nations* and *Discovering and Embracing God's Global Purpose* Bible studies, *Real Life Series* of missions issues brochures, and the popular *Trail Guide Map*!

- Unreached People Resources. Tools to aid people in their understanding of unreached peoples and how to pray for them. Items include Prayer Cards, books like *Operation World*, and more!

- Children's Products. Include the popular *Kids Around the World* series of videos and curriculum supplements designed to expose kids to unreached peoples and how they might be involved in reaching them for Christ. This range also includes the top children's resources recommended by Caleb Project's children's ministries department.

- Caleb Project often partners with missions agencies and churches to train research teams and create media tools to help mobilize others. We have a full-time staff of professional print, video, and digital media producers. If you are considering putting together a team and would like to talk with Caleb Project about a potential partnership, please contact us at *info@cproject.com*.

For current prices and ordering information, please contact Caleb Project.

10 West Dry Creek Circle
Littleton, CO 80120-4413
303.730.4170 • 303.730.4177 – Fax
info@cproject.com • *www.calebproject.org*

Appendix III:
People Specific Advocacy

After we had been doing research for some years, we found some of our team members being called to continue learning about and the waving the flag for the peoples they had researched. God was leading them into a ministry of "advocacy," learning, praying, and networking to see more resources directed toward the people they had come to love. Please consider if advocacy might be a logical extension of your research, as well.

What is a People-Group Advocate?

The advocate works with others to help bridge the gap between a specific people group and specific resources within the global kingdom of God. The advocate becomes a voice for the cause of an unreached people. He or she may be a cultural learner, a relationship nurturer and networker, and an activist or champion. Each people group has somewhat different needs, and each advocate has somewhat different personality, gifting, and calling, so this ministry can take place any number of ways. Increasingly, strategic partnerships, research, and the same sort of thinking that mission leaders have been using to develop plans for reaching unreached people groups are being applied to serving local ethnic populations, as well.

If you are interested in becoming an advocate for a specific unreached people group, please write or call Caleb Project or one of the organizations listed below.

Learning More

Keys to the Nations: Unlocking Doors to the Unreached draws articles from a variety of sources about unreached peoples, people-group advocacy, adopting people groups, partnership and networking, security issues, fundraising, and prayer. Littleton, CO: Caleb Project, 2001 (new expanded edition).

A number of the resources in *Keys to the Nations* appear in AD2000's Adoption Guidance Program, which focuses on the relationship between local churches and ministries to unreached peoples. This is no longer updated but is still available on-line (*www.ad2000.org/adoption*). To connect with others who share your interest in a people group, talk to the staff of Joshua Project II which is actively collecting data about the unreached and work among them.

Joshua Project II
PO Box 64080
Colorado Springs, CO 80962 USA
719.785.0120
info@joshuaproject.net
www.joshuaproject.net

Forming Partnerships

Interdev's partnership training courses provides specific and specialized training for potential partnership facilitators. The most popular course, now offered worldwide in English, French, and Arabic includes 4-5 days of training in how to develop an interest in partnership among potential partners, preparing to bring potential partners together in a meeting, managing the process in a partnership meeting, building consensus among diverse ministries, and understanding conflict in partnerships.

Interdev US office
PO Box 3883
Seattle, WA 98124 USA
425.775.8330
idev-us@interdev.org

Interdev UK Office
PO Box 210
West Drayton, Middlesex UB7 8NN UK
+44.1895.438321
training@interdev.org.uk

Train to be a Strategy Coordinator

The Southern Baptist Convention's International Mission Board, the Cooperative Baptist Fellowship, and Youth With a Mission's People-Group Advocate Program all train full-time workers to serve as "Strategy Coordinators." The opportunities for a full-time advocate are intense and endless; all the more reason to pursue them in the context of a supportive environment that allows you to learn from those who have gone before!

Excerpts from several great resources from the International Mission Board, David Garrison's classic book *The Non-Residential Missionary* and his more recent booklet *Church-Planting Movements*, are also included in *Keys to the Nations. Church-Planting Movements* is a must-read, and can be viewed on-line at *www.imb.org/CPM.*

International Mission Board, SBC
PO Box 6767
Richmond, VA 23230-0767 USA
800.866.3621
www.imb.org
nomads@pobox.com

Cooperative Baptist Fellowship
PO Box 450329
Atlanta, GA 31145-0329 USA
770.220.1600
fellowship@cbfnet.org
www.cbfonline.org

YWAM Frontier Missions Office
Highfield Oval, Harpenden
Hertsfordshire England AL54BX UK
+44.1582.463300
ico@oval.com

Appendix IV:
Recruiting Profiles

Research Expedition Teams

Team Profile

The following team profile can be used to guide selection of team members for a research expedition. Each team member participates in field research, yet some team members provide additional expertise in specific areas. One team member may fill more than one role. On a well-rounded team, members complement one another so that all of these roles are fulfilled.

Photographer – one who can capture unreached people on film for use in prayer guides.

Worship Leader – one with gifts and experience to effectively lead the team in corporate worship.

Treasurer – one who can responsibly keep track of team finances.

Computer Coordinator – one who can train and coach the team in their use of computers and printers and keep a system up and running.

Intercessor – one with a special burden, gifting, and vision for intercession, leading the team by example in prayer.

Encourager – one with exhortation gifts who naturally lifts and encourages the team in the midst of a difficult task.

Counselor – one who assists the team leader in ministering to those who may have specific spiritual or interpersonal struggles on the expedition.

Cheerleader – one who enjoys planning activities and days off and who effectively includes the serious or lonely types.

Project Captains – those who can responsibly supervise a team sub-project such as writing a prayer guide, creating media tools, or coordinating living and eating arrangements.

Team Member Profile

Qualified team members should demonstrate maturity and ability in the following areas: spiritual life, analytical skills, academics, and overseas experience.

Spiritual Life

Team members should be pursuing a vital, growing relationship with God. Team members should be prepared to live in a spiritually oppressive environment. Each person can expect spiritual struggle, perhaps even with their own faith and convictions. A strong and tested faith is necessary to meet these challenges.

A prayer support team, usually from one's home church, is vital for team members. Researchers should be actively involved in the life of a church.

A team member should also have a growing commitment to world evangelization. That is, each one should be open to fulfill whatever role God may have for them. Each should be committed to stewardship of the exposure and information obtained on the expedition. He or she must be motivated primarily by obedience and love for Jesus, not the thrill of adventure or the romance of overseas travel.

Analytical Skills

A well developed ability to think critically is a necessary skill for team members to be successful. Ethnographic research is essentially a problem solving activity. While experience in sociological or anthropological research can be helpful, it is not necessary. However, an ability to analyze problems and work toward potential solutions is essential. Team members must be able to read and digest material at the college level. They must be able to comprehend and contribute in the areas of missiology and ethnography.

Writing Skills

Clear and concise writing skills are essential. Team members take daily notes of their conversations and then type them on lap top computers. A mid-summary report is written in addition to a final strategy report. Video scripts, prayer guides, and other mobilization tools are also written.

Academics

No specific major or area of study is required. However, two years of college is usually the minimum requirement to insure the necessary academic skills and maturity. We also require team members to take the missions study course *Perspectives on the World Christian Movement.*

Experience

Previous cross-cultural experience is recommended. This type of expedition is not designed to be an initial exposure to missions. Experience in teamwork and research are also helpful.

As with any cross-cultural endeavor, a successful team member will also have a high tolerance for ambiguity. This quality enables them to "roll with the punches" of overseas living. Each team member will need to go beyond surviving culture shock to producing strategic research. Team members will pursue relationships with nationals, learning to appreciate and relate to them.

Age and Marital Status

Most expedition team members are between 23 and 30 years old. However, maturity, not age, is the guideline. While most team members are single, married couples and young families are welcome. We find they often lend stability to the team situation.

Team Leader Profile

Leadership and Overseas Experience

The team leader should have experience caring for a group of people and providing oversight and direction for the completion of a project. The team leader should be an active, committed member of a local church. He should be involved in leadership in a church body and have a proven record of working effectively with and serving others.

We also strongly recommend that a team leader have some cross-cultural experience. Without it, he may have difficulty leading others through the experience. He must have an appreciation for and understanding of cultures different from his own.

Relational Skills

The team leader must be effective and insightful regarding interpersonal relationships. He should be willing to confront others, as well as show care and compassion in a Christ-like way. This position calls for a person who enjoys a great deal of interaction with people. The team leader role requires empathy for others. He must earn the trust of team members and coach them in effective team relationships.

Spiritual Maturity

The team leader should maintain a strong spiritual walk that is reflected in his daily life. Team members must be able to trust him to lead for God's glory, not his own. He should give spiritual input and exhort the team when appropriate.

Character

The team leader should enjoy breaking new ground, be highly motivated, and be capable of dealing with ambiguity. The team leader must be able to inspire confidence and command respect. He should be a self starter and team player, able to motivate himself and his team. Servanthood and personal maturity are also essential character qualities.

Research

The team leader does not need to be a research expert. A working knowledge of missiology and church planting, however, is helpful. The team leader can work with a research coordinator to carry out the research.

Mobilization

The team leader should be able to mobilize team members to further involvement in missions. In a disciple-like relationship, the leader can pose challenging questions and seek to instill greater vision in team members. He may also help guide the team in setting mobilization goals and developing tools that will motivate the church toward evangelization of the unreached.

Marriage/Family status

The team leader can be married or single. There is great strength in having a husband and wife as a leadership team. On the other hand, qualified single men have proven quite successful as team leaders. If married, the wife should be fully supportive of this ministry, owning it herself, not just "going along for the ride."

She can contribute a great deal in all areas of team leadership. Couples with children may find it too difficult to lead a research team and care for their family in such a rigorous situation.

Glossary

Foreign Words

Many of these words can be spelled more than one way in English. The spelling and pronunciation guides we have used are our best attempt to spell them clearly. Also, in some cases, the language of origin may be questionable. We have provided the information based on limited exposure to these languages.

aksakal	Kazakh. (**ahk**-sah-kahl) Translated, "White beard." An aksakal is an older man in leadership who is valued and honored for his wisdom.
aytis	Kazakh. (**eye**-teez) Ancient tradition; a poetry-singing competition.
barami	Thai. (bah-**rah**-mee) Respect and devotion given to a Thai leader which increases as the number of his followers grows.
basti	Urdu. (**bahs**-tee) Slum communities settled by recent immigrants to Indian cities.
batu	Bahasa Indonesia. (**bah**-too) Literally, "stone." The game of dominoes.
bomoh	Bahasa Malaysia. (**boh**-mah) Traditional animistic folk healer.
bourkas	(**buhr**-kahz) A head covering worn by many Indian Muslim women.
bumiputra	Bahasa Malaysia. (**boo**-mee-**poo**-trah) Literally, "son of the soil." Preferred status given to indigenous Malays over citizens of Chinese and Indian descent.
chatur	Bahasa Indonesia. (**chah**-tuhr) The game of chess.
choikhonas	Uzbek. (choy-**hoh**-nahz) Tea houses.
dim sum	Chinese. (**dihm**-suhm) A Chinese dumpling.

ethne	Greek. (**ehth**-nay) Of or pertaining to a race, nation, or people group.
gecekondus	Turkish or Kurdish. (**gehch**-ee-**kahn**-dooz) Shanties built by migrants, often overnight, on someone else's unguarded property.
goothdigme	Turkmen. (gooth-**dihg**-may) The evil eye, a bad spirit or a curse.
Isaan	Thai. (**ee**-sahn) A tribal group living in northeastern Thailand.
jalan	Bahasa Malaysia. (**jah**-lahn) Literally, "road." Figurative use "*jalan, jalan*" means "not going anywhere in particular."
kairos	Greek. (**keye**-rohs) A seasonable time or opportunity. Often used to describe a time of openness or potential breakthrough in spiritual work.
kampung	Bahasa Malaysia or Indonesia. (**kahm**-puhng) A tightly-knit traditional Malay or Indonesian neighborhood.
Kirmanji	Kurdish. (kehr-**mahn**-jee) One of several Kurdish language dialects.
losmens	Bahasa Indonesia. (**lohs**-mehns) Boarding houses similar to youth hostels.
manat	Turkmen. (mah-**naht**) Currency used in Turkmenistan after they gained independence in 1992.
muhalla	Arabic. (moo-**hah**-lah) A traditional neighborhood where extended family often live together in one house.
mullah	Arabic. (**moo**-lah) Muslim religious leader trained in traditional law and doctrine.
nan	Arabic. (**nahn**) Round, flat bread.
oman	Arabic. (oh-**mahn**) Prayer.
pilau	Turkish. (pih-**lahw**) A rice dish served with meat and/or vegetables.
pos	Bahasa Indonesia. (**pohs**) An elevated shack where young men gather to socialize.
Qur'an	(kuhr-**ahn**) Muslim holy book.
rantau	Bahasa Indonesia. (rahn-**tahw**) A journey to the city made by young men looking for better jobs.
rida	Gujarati. (**ree**-dah) The type of compulsory dress worn by Bohra women. Often brightly colored.

sunet	Turkish. (soo-**neht**) Ceremony and celebration of a boy's circumcision between ages five and ten.
Syedna	Unknown. (seye-**ehd**-nah) Highest religious leader of the Bohras.
taman	Bahasa Malaysia. (**tah**-mahn) Modern urban neighborhood.
tebip	Kazakh. (teh-**beeb**) A magician with healing powers.
Thai-jin	Thai. (**teye**-jihn) A person of mixed Chinese-Thai ethnicity.
Thai-teh	Thai. (**teye**-teh) A "true-Thai" or ethnic Thai as opposed to a citizen of Thailand of Chinese or tribal descent.
zhuz	Kazakh. (**zhoos**) Tribe.

Missiological Words

These words are often defined in different ways in the mission community. The words are defined below as we have used them in the text.

church planting	The ministry which focuses on establishing new churches, in contrast to other kinds of ministries focused on other goals such as Bible translation, relief efforts, literature and radio evangelism, etc.
contextualization	Adapting the message, messenger, and the church so as to make it relevent to a given context.
envisioning	A perspective which develops church-planting strategy by beginning with the end in mind. And an activity which involves trying to determine what the end might look like so that a strategy can be developed.
evangelism	The activity of sharing the gospel with an individual or group.
evangelization	The resulting state of a group or individual who has heard and understood the gospel. We use this term to refer primarily to sociological groups.
FOQUS	An acronym for the research cycle. F=Focus, O=Observe, Q=Question, U=Understand, and S=Strategize.
indigenous	When a church reflects the culture of its native people.
mobilization	The process of moving an individual or group toward greater involvement in fulfilling the Great Commission.
people group	The largest group of people within which the gospel can spread

as a church-planting movement without encountering barriers of acceptance or understanding.

people movement	Refers to a widespread response to the gospel among a people group.
prayerwalking	Praying on-site with insight.
reached	A people group in which there is a viable church capable of evangelizing the rest of the group.
receptivity	Degree of openness, particularly to the gospel message.
strategizing	Using current information to plan for the future.
targeting	Selecting one group or individual among many; to choose a focus.
unreached	A people group lacking a viable church capable of evangelizing the rest of the group.
tentmakers	Missionary workers who are secularly employed overseas.
worker	Missionary.
world view	One's way of looking at the world including deeply held assumptions about the nature of reality.

Ethnographic Words

The words below have more precise and scientific definitions in textbooks and reference works. We have provided a simple definition based on how the word is used in this manual.

boundary maintenance	The actions taken to include group members and exclude others.
crystallization	The result of converging similarities that spontaneously strike ethnographers as relevant or important to their study.
cultural helper	A person who helps you understand their culture through their eyes.
domestic group	Individuals who pool economic resources and cooperate in the performance of domestic activities: shopping, cooking, eating, cleaning, laundry, and child care.
emic	An insider's perspective of a culture or society.
enculturation	Being thoroughly familiar with a culture.

ethnography	The work of describing a culture from a native point of view.
etic	An outsider's pespective of a culture or society.
group allegiance	A sense of connection with group members characterized by loyalty to one another.
impression management	When cultural helpers tell you what they think you want to hear. A subtle skewing of information.
networks	Relationship webs made up of individuals that a cultural helper knows and interacts with.
participant observation	The ethnographic skill of watching while doing.
rapport	Refers to a harmonious relationship between a cultural helper and ethnographer which allows for the free flow of information.
social dynamics	Forces which affect the social evolution of a particular people group.
social identity	A sense of group uniqueness based on similarity to one another and distinction from others.
social stratification	Boundaries between significant population segments.
social structure	How members of a people group relate to others inside and outside the group.
taxonomies	A set of categories organized on the basis of a term or idea important to the members of a people group.
teamlet partners	A pair of ethnographers.
trolling	Walking the streets to find new cultural helpers.
validation	Testing one source of information against another to prove a hypothesis.
verification	Checking with others to confirm your analysis and interpretation of research findings.

References

Adeney, Dr. Miriam. *Cultural Research Questions*. A list given to seminar participants, n.d.

Barrett, David B. and Todd M. Johnson. *Our Globe and How to Reach It*. Birmingham, AL: New Hope, 1990.

Brewster, Dr. Thomas and Elizabeth S. Brewster. *Language Acquisition Made Practical: Field Methods for Language Learners*. Pasadena, CA: Lingua House, 1976.

Cage, John. *The International Thesaurus of Quotations*. New York: Harper and Row, 1987.

Covey, Steven R. *The Seven Habits of Highly Effective People*. New York: Simon and Schuster, 1989.

Eames, Edwin and Judith Granich Goode. *Anthropology of the City: An Introduction to Urban Anthropology*. Englewood Cliffs, NJ: Prentice-Hall, 1977.

Fetterman, David M. *Ethnography Step by Step*. Newbury Park, CA: SAGE Publications, 1989.

Garrison, V. David. *The Nonresidential Missionary*. Monrovia, CA: MARC, 1990

Gibson, Tim, Steven C. Hawthorne, Richard Krekel, and Ken Moy. *Stepping Out: A Guide to Short-term Missions*. Seattle, WA: YWAM Publishing, 1996.

Hawthorne, Steve and Graham Kendrick. *Prayerwalking: Praying On-site with Insight*. Lake Mary, FL: Creation House, 1993.

Into All the World: The Annual Great Commission Opportunities Handbook. Pasadena, CA: Berry Publishing.

Johnstone, Patrick. *People Groups: How Many Are Unreached?* Pasadena, CA: International Journal of Frontier Missions, 1990.

Jorgensen, Danny L. *Participant Observation: A Methodology for Human Studies.* Newbury Park, CA: SAGE Publications, 1989.

McKinney, Carol. *Globe Trotting in Sandals: Culture Research Field Methods Guide.* Dallas, TX: SIL, 1992.

Reaching the Peoples of Bangkok. Pasadena, CA: Caleb Project, 1988.

Robb, John D. *Focus! The Power of People Group Thinking.* Monrovia, CA: MARC, 1989, 1994.

Smith, Alex G. *Siamese Gold: The Church in Thailand.* Bangkok, Thailand: Kanok Bannasan (OMF Publishers), 1981.

Spradley, James P. *The Ethnographic Interview.* New York: Holt, Rinehart and Winston, 1979.

Spradley, James P. *Participant Observation.* New York: Holt, Rinehart and Winston, 1980.

Winter, Dr. Ralph D. and Steven C. Hawthorne, eds. Perspectives on the World Christian Movement: A Reader. Pasadena, CA: William Carey Library, 1999.

For more information on the *Perspectives* Study Program, see *www.perspectives.org*.

Index

Notes

Notes

Notes

Notes

Notes

Notes

Notes